Studio: Asia

Studio:Asia

Written and Illustrated by JOHN GROTH

THE WORLD

PUBLISHING COMPANY

CLEVELAND AND NEW YORK

FIRST EDITION

Library of Congress Catalog Card Number: 52-5195

We are grateful to the following organizations for permission to use material included in this book: *Abbott Laboratories, Metropolitan Group, Argosy Magazine, and Esquire Magazine.* Special thanks to Jane Miller, without whose editorial assistance this book could not have been completed and to Pan-American World Airways pilots for getting me to Asia and back in safety and comfort.

CC 952

CONTENTS

To Ann

Introduction

I went to Asia because I hoped to extend the deep experience I had shared with American GI's, Normandy farmers, Parisian artists and the other people in Europe caught up in World War II.

I have always drawn and painted people in action. I am a genre painter. I have sketched jockeys Eddie Arcaro and Ted Atkinson at Belmont; Joe Louis and Ezzard Charles in training camp; Jackie Robinson taking his cut in the Dodgers' batting cage; the horse buyers in the Chicago stockyards; the football team in scrimmage at Notre Dame. I have drawn people at play on the beaches and in the parks of great cities; people in the streets of New York's East Side and Chicago's West Side.

I went to Asia, basically, to draw people. I was richly rewarded.

I will never forget the terrible poignancy of a whole country in flight, lines of Korean refugees moving against a background of burning homes, old men gasping for breath, children held at mothers' icy breasts. There was, for me, the special heartbreak of a small Korean boy whom I found dying in a deserted village. I could not take him with me. And the accusation in the eyes of the Indo-Chinese mother in a battle-wrecked village. I offered a bar of chocolate to her child: she flung it back at me in contempt.

Of course, there were happier moments in Asia. I delighted in the charming children of the Japanese countryside who knew me as "Bubble Gum-san." My months on a Japanese farm formed perhaps my warmest Asia memory. The Iwamotos treated me with the extreme considerateness of a weekend guest though I stayed for months. I still smile over the image of Mama-san, calmly eating the entire pint jar of peanut butter I had given her, with a spoon at one sitting, as though it was a pint of ice cream. Symbol of the family's devotion to me was Ondori-san, the one legged rooster who moved into my studio at the farm and served as combination gentleman's companion and substitute alarm clock.

There are some unforgettable figures in my Asiatic portfolio: Cecilia, the amateur artist who invited me to her bordello-home to criticize her drawings; Martin, the terribly wounded British lieutenant who fought bravely for survival with the help of a wonderful doctor on the Danish hospital ship Jutlandia.

There was the slightly demented side of Asia. In Hong Kong, I choked my way through a snake dinner that cost $10 a plate, beginning with a soup in which bits of snakeskin floated. The companion who initiated me to opium ate fried milk as a hangover remedy. I met a tribesman's wife in the Kyber Pass who had a mail order nose. (Her husband had sliced hers off because she had been unfaithful.) I saw a Buddhist priest light his cigarette and his shrine candles from the flame of an American Zippo lighter. A Tokyo Geisha, who looked as though she had stepped out of a 17th century block print, smacked me heartily on the back with a "Hi-ya, Joe!"

I also got a charge from the parrot pet of a French battalion stationed on the Indo-China defense perimeter who spurned powdered wine and drank only Burgundy.

In Korea, I found that every UN soldier to whom I talked had his own motive for fighting the Communists. The Canadians, Australians and Dutch used words like "adventure" and "sport." I was willing to believe it of them, too. "Aussies" insisted upon wearing their famous bush hats into battle. One severely wounded man refused to go into an operating room until he was permitted to take his hat with him.

The Greeks and Turks were most serious about "their" war. "We're here to fight Communism." I saw a fanatical Greek soldier in a field hospital who had to be bodily prevented by nurses and corpsmen from attacking a North Korean POW on another stretcher.

American GI's evaded answering why they were there. One private tossed it right back at me with a terse, "You tell me, Mac!" Despite their seeming cynicism, however, they sweated out the worst of the war, draped in blankets, as they hugged isolated posts on icy mountain peaks. They wise-cracked their way out of their own wretchedness, describing themselves as "perfect *Life* covers."

They notably wore the biggest hearts in Korea. Every battalion had its Korean orphan mascots. I witnessed a parting scene between a grizzled sergeant and his "adopted" boy. The child held an enormous burden of candy, gum and toys, but he was crying as though his heart would break as he gazed up at the sergeant. I didn't hang around: the sergeant wasn't so dry-eyed himself.

GI's, led by a gallant little captain from Perth Amboy, New Jersey, started a hospital in Pusan for the sick and maimed children of Korea. Everyone pitched in to help. MP's commandeered supplies. Sailors in the harbor made toys. GI's in the area gave mess rations and candy. A water supply sergeant delivered a daily tankload of water. A Negro mess sergeant supervised the cooking. All of this on their off duty time.

The American field hospitals never turned away a sick or injured Korean, man, woman or child. I saw a little Korean girl with an ugly, festering wound enter a field receiving tent at a time when battle casualties were pouring in. She was treated as tenderly as though she were a top general.

My physical mementos of Asia are few. I carry a rent in the skirt of my trenchcoat from an overenthusiastic re-enactment of a French bayonet charge. A scorch on my musette bag reminds me of a predawn fire in an overheated Korean hut. There is a faint, sweet odor of damp rot from Hong Kong that clings to the pages of my books and sketch pads.

To others, such things may be trivial, but to me they evoke the unforgettable year when my studio was Asia.

THE AUTHOR

1 · Blood for Korea

Korea began for me when a wooden box bearing the dramatic legend HUMAN BLOOD was unloaded in an ice-cold dawn at Taegu airport. The box and I had flown ten thousand miles since leaving San Francisco three days and nights before. The mission that brought me to Asia had started at the Red Cross Bank in San Francisco when I gave my blood along with a group of clerks, shopkeepers and housewives. I was to record in words and pictures the giving of our blood, the transportation of it and the administering of it to wounded men at the Korea end.

With proper male instinct I had seated myself next to Shirley Ann Novak, pretty brunette stenographer, in the Red Cross waiting room. I softened the curious-suspicious glance she gave my uniform by explaining I was the war correspondent who was acting as courier for the much-publicized blood delivery to Korea. I told her I was leaving the next morning. Shirley countered with, "I have a guy in Korea. That's why *I'm* here." That put everything in its proper perspective. As we chatted with the other donors-to-be, we found they had men in Korea also. Nurse Hilda Platt's husband was stationed at Pusan. This morning she was in the dual role of nurse and donor.

A bespectacled clerk boasted seven cousins in Korea. Liquor officer Jack Maloney included himself in the group having relatives on the fighting front.

"I donated twenty-three times. I consider anybody walking around with my blood in them my kin."

I was the only near casualty of the morning. I came close to throwing a faint when the tube was pulled from my arm. Nurses rushing Bourbon saved me from disgracing my martial costume.

While cameras flashed, I lettered "JG" on the label of my container. It was packed with the bottles of the other donors. I would join the box at the airport.

Korea-bound paratroopers exchanged significant glances when they read the box's legend as it was being loaded aboard the Pan American Clipper. They were flying on another ship—for psychological reasons, blood and soldiers are flown separately. A few minutes later, the Clipper took off like an angry stork.

At Honolulu's airport, crowds of weary women and children sat on piles of luggage. The families of men stationed in Eastern trouble zones, they were being shipped home. Other returning travelers were gray-faced Korean veterans, who were sweating out priorities. At Wake Island I saw the paratroopers again. Hunched under heavy packs, they looked like black question marks against the spotlights of the airfield.

We were guided into Haneda airport by a radio beam. A thick gray fog muffled Tokyo. The box was rushed to necessary refrigeration. I jeeped into Tokyo for credentials and winter gear.

I could see little of Nippon through the mist. My first impressions disappointed me. It was not the charming Japan of wood-block prints—no pagoda-like temples or bright kimono-clad girls. Instead, I saw only dreary wooden shacks and bare stone structures that differed but little from a Midwest industrial suburb. But for Japanese characters on signs, I might have been in Toledo or Gary. The girls I saw were well hidden by shapeless raincoats. I reserved judgment, however. I knew I would be back many times in the months ahead.

10

The soldier-blood taboo was disregarded on the Korea hop. The box sat with stacks of bedrolls in the aisle. The men in bucket seats paid it scant attention.

Most of the soldiers were asleep in their parka hoods before we passed Fujiyama's symbolic cone. This was my first close look at soldiers in this war. The sophisticated Americans were doing most of the sleeping. Bush-hatted Australians loudly recounted Tokyo girl adventures, while British soldiers, whose steep-peaked garrison caps bit into their noses, listened. Freshly arrived Belgian officers sat erect and eyed everyone and everything with interest. The smallest of them was especially incongruous among the carelessly draped forms of the other UN soldiers. He wore an impeccably tailored uniform. There was a monocle in his eye and he held a swagger stick and a miniature camera.

Belgium Officers
on C 47 to Changjin

"Frozen Chosen" welcomed us with a crackling twenty degrees below zero. We kept our feet with difficulty in the cutting wind that knifed down from icy ridges. The explosive sound of Thunder Jets taking off from Taegu's airfield tore the air, as they carried jellied gasoline and bombs to enemy-held mountains. Fur-hatted South Koreans loaded the box of blood onto a weapons carrier. I chinned myself aboard as it moved off.

11

Numbing cold smarted my eyes as the open truck bounced over the frozen dirt road and bleared the outlines of the tanks, trucks, and ox carts we passed.

We wheeled into the courtyard of a schoolhouse turned hospital. The Japanese had built schoolhouses in every Korean village and town during their occupation of the country. They were the biggest and best-constructed buildings in most towns. They were used by UN forces as hospitals, headquarters and barracks.

Cooperative corpsmen arranged for the blood to be used almost immediately. Within an hour it was entering the veins of men who needed it.

Private James Herbert of Bessemer, Ala., his head and chest wrapped in bandages, was reading *Captain Marvel* as he received blood from the box. Another comic book, *Cat Woman,* rested on his chest. He had just undergone his third operation since he had been wounded in an uphill assault. Exploding grenades had sent fragments into his chest, side and head.

The young Negro private was unaware of my purpose in talking to him but like most wounded soldiers, he didn't mind a break from bed monotony. After telling me how he had been wounded, he talked eagerly of home, which was not far off for him.

I asked him how he felt about the blood he was receiving.

"It's real life blood to me. It's what is getting me home. Without it, I wouldn't be alive and able to read these stories," he said, pointing to the comic books.

In another bed, in what had once been a kindergarten room, lay tiny Corporal Eleuterio Perez. The Puerto Rican smiled under his turban-sized bandage, as I approached. He had received his blood during an operation a few minutes before. He had been shot in the head. He showed me his war souvenir, a GI issue pile cap. He poked his finger through two burnt-edged holes, one in the back flap, the other in the left ear flap. He explained that the bullet passed through the edge of his skull.

"Good thing, or I still have it in my head," was his comment. "My two baby would have no father."

12

In another room Private Ali Ugar of Elâziz, Turkey, too ill to talk, was receiving his life-giving fluid in an oxygen tent, but his friends, gold-toothed Sergeant Sein Drahor of Istanbul and midget-sized Private Zeynal Kavlach of Ankara, were eager to talk of him and show me the Chinese bullet taken from Ali's chest.

Aidemen laid a boy in a bed nearby, and strapped a bottle bearing my initials above him. His face was whiter than the pillow. Within a few minutes, my blood brought color to his pallid cheeks. He opened his eyes and asked who I was.

I told him but did not mention my connection with him. I hesitated to fatigue him with talk after the hour-long operation he had endured, but he asked me to please stay.

"Really it helps," he said.

He told me he was Private Larry Turk from Brooklyn. He spoke at length of the action in which he had received his chest wound.

13

"The whole company was retreating through some woods near the 38th Parallel. It was night. Suddenly we were ambushed. The enemy was shooting all around us and we couldn't see anyone to shoot at. I was hit. I lay face down on the snow, hurting. When the shooting stopped, everyone was gone except five of us who were wounded, and lying close to each other. It was no use calling

for help, there was nobody near. I prayed all that night and the next day. Along about midnight, Chinese soldiers came up to us. We played dead. They turned me over with their guns but I held my breath. They jerked the cap off my head and took my gloves. One of the gloves was covered with blood. They went away without giving us a 'burst.' All the next day I wondered if we'd ever be picked up. I don't know why I didn't bleed to death. Guess because it was so cold. Must have froze my wounds shut. Just before dark on the second day, medics came up and took us away."

Larry's buddy joined us, Private Joe Cooper, Valdese, N. C. He announced that he was ready to write Mrs. Turk for Larry. He addressed an envelope, first asking Larry his mother's first name and Brooklyn street number. Larry was silent as Joe wrote steadily, page after page. I wondered if telepathy was taking place in front of me. Finally, I asked Joe how he knew what Larry wanted to say in the letter.

"Oh, that's easy. I'm writing the same letter I wrote my own mother this morning. All mothers like to hear the same thing."

Larry concurred, "Ma said the last one was the best letter I ever wrote."

Every few minutes a soldier would pop his head in the doorway to ask Larry "Howya doin', Turk?" Each time, the Turkish soldiers around Ali Ugar's bed wheeled around expectantly. Wondering why Larry was in a ward with Turks instead of Americans I asked him "How come?"

He laughed for the first time since I had been in the room.

"When they unloaded me, the corpsmen saw 'Turk' on my tag and put me in here with them. They're good Joes. I'm teaching 'em English, Brooklyn style. They'll be Dodger fans before I leave!"

His face was animated now. His cheeks had color. I thought about the dark woods of the 38th Parallel, the frozen ground on which he had lain, the Communist bayonets that had cruelly prodded him, his matter-of-fact courage. I was glad that Larry Turk had received my blood. I wished that the others who had given their blood could have had my experience of seeing it bring new life to a wounded man who needed it.

2 · Snowmen on the Mountains

Air Force General Vandenberg was pilot on my first flight over enemy territory. There were a few harrowing moments when I thought it would be my first and last view of Central Korea.

I had been waiting several hours at Taegu's icy airport for a ride north to Chung-ju when General Hoyt Vandenberg arrived with an escort of lesser generals. He remembered me from Normandy days. General Van asked if I would like to go along on a sightseeing flight over enemy lines. He offered to drop me at Chung-ju on the return flight. I was delighted. That was my destination—the Second Division held a front line north of the city. Enemy attacks were expected against their lines. I hoped to find there the action I had come to Korea to see.

Each general was furnished a parka and a pair of expensive fur-lined flight boots for the cold trip. I was given a pair which I wrapped in my bedroll, saving them for the freezing jeep trips ahead.

It was a smooth flight up to the mountains beyond the Han River. Generals at windows were soon bored with ice-covered mountains, however. They were eager to see one live enemy soldier.

At this point General Van took over the controls. He threw the plane into a dive and hedge-hopped in an effort to find the enemy. We snaked through narrow valleys, scraping wing tips on rock faces and brushing fir tops, without flushing so much as a rabbit. Enemy experience with American planes had sent every living thing above ground to cover.

He buzzed roads and farmhouses in reckless disregard of the precious cargo of high brass in the cabin behind him. He was remarkably able with the stick even though his last few years had been spent in a Pentagon command chair. I prayed for sight of an enemy soldier. I think I would have welcomed ack-ack fire—it might have terminated the game of aerial leapfrog. With their white uniforms against the snow, we might not have seen the North Koreans anyway. Sometimes we were so close to the ground that if the wheels had not been retracted, we would have made a landing.

16

General Van finally gave up. The landing at Chung-ju shook us like popcorn. It was not the fault of the pilot. The air field was covered with foot-high frozen ruts. A row of planes, damaged in landings, lay along one side of the field, their wings and fusilages twisted and broken.

The General and an aide immediately climbed into a helicopter. I was invited to come along but quickly refused. The handsome, boyish general looked genuinely disappointed but I was not eager for another game of leap frog at even closer range. This time the General might get close enough to look into slanted black eyes and count the cartridges in their belts.

A waiting press jeep took me to Second Division headquarters. The snow-covered plains on either side of the Han were treeless. Houses were broken and burned. Roads were muddy streams that tunneled through dust-stained snowbanks. Huddles of soldiers crouched over fires. Lines of white-clad refugees were barely distinguishable in the snow that had begun to fall. Engineers, hip-deep in ice water, were repairing the pontoon bridge over which we crossed the Han.

Twilight was purpling the landscape as our jeep dipped into a small valley. Divisional CP was in a village at its far end. A spectral light was thrown over the village by a small mountain of hay and manure that was burning like a miniature Vesuvius.

The press was in a schoolhouse. My entry was greeted with mixed curses and shouts of "Shut the door" and "It's ten below in here already!"

The room was freezing. Most of the war reporters hugged a potbelly stove on which beans and coffee sputtered. The crowded scene of bearded men in overalls, red sweaters and checked woolen shirts and stocking caps reminded me for a moment of a Quebec lumber camp I had visited. Every correspondent is issued a field uniform. However, as civilians, they can exercise personal tastes. Some startling combinations result. Bright red hunting shirts are worn over baggy paratrooper pants, orange mufflers over surrealist-patterned ski sweaters. Helmets are discarded for red deer-hunting caps and black caracul fezzes. I joined the sartorial parade with a French paratrooper beret and imperial beard.

There was little headline writing though two heroic souls finger-stabbed at portables amidst a din of argument and a French correspondent shrieked in Gallic over a field telephone. Underneath him, reporters played cards on a blanket.

Bearded Jack Thompson of the *Chicago Tribune,* whom I had not seen since Paris Liberation days, broke open a case of Scotch in my honor. The whiskey won me instant acceptance.

I was billeted in a tiny thatch-roofed hut on the other side of the Vesuvius stack. My roommate was a big, rangy, good-natured Australian, Warren White of Reuter's. The hut was heated by an underfloor oven stoked from the outside with pine branches. The floor was warm. Sometimes we slept on it. Occasionally, the overheated ovens would ignite houses. I was awakened several times by shouts of "Fire!"

Toward dawn the fires invariably died and we awoke in a room crackling with subarctic cold. It required real courage to leave the sleeping bags though we had slept in our clothes. We frantically added more wool—stockings, sweaters, mufflers, parkas—and wound up looking like three-hundred-pounders.

Breakfast deadline was six-thirty. Usually late-arriving correspondents tripped and fell over icy ridges while they ran and fastened trousers in an effort to make it before the door was shut by an iron-willed mess sergeant.

The cold was felt most severely in the officers' latrine. It was covered by a tent of non-cold-resistant canvas. One morning a colonel gasped to me, "I feel like a hero every time I drop my pants—from the cold, *of course!"*

A friendly card game on my first night cost me most of my Korean money and travelers' checks. The sergeant who won it attempted to mitigate my shorn feelings by giving me a lead on what he considered a story.

The next morning he guided me to a group of farm buildings outside the village. Squat South Korean police were questioning suspected farmer-guerrillas. One of the farmers, who had already been questioned, lay face down on the stone slabs of the yard. Another who was in the process of being questioned was tied to a post. As he was held erect by a policeman grasping him by the hair, another hit him about the face with a leather-covered club. When he sank to his knees, they shouted questions at him. He made no answer and they repeated the beating. He fainted. They dashed cold water on him but he did not revive. He was dead.

The sergeant told me that both the men were to have been shot, in any event, at three that afternoon. If I wanted to watch the execution of the surviving suspect, I was welcome to do so. I declined. Thinking I was disappointed in the show, he promised another interrogation of suspects that I would find more interesting. The beautiful mistress of the police chief—I had seen the Korean girl striding about camp in slacks and boots (she carried a .45)—assisted at important examinations. If the suspect refused to talk, he was held spread-eagled on the ground while she kicked at his testicles until he did. I declined this show, too.

We were briefed nightly by G-2 officers. From the information we were given, we planned our next day's work. The entire front was static and there was little activity aside from patrols, though according to the headlines that grew out of correspondents' stories by the time they reached the states, you would have thought whole divisions were in action rather than patrols.

While waiting for large-scale action, I visited the American units in the mountains directly ahead of us and planned trips to the French, Dutch, and British.

This was a tougher war to cover than the European campaign of '44 and '45. It meant long jeep rides in blizzardy mountain passes and tortuous hikes up steel slopes to reach men in isolated outposts. The precious fur-lined flight boots I had saved for the jeep trips were a great disappointment. When I put them on, I found they were both for the left foot. I gave them to a Korean orderly.

On the long climbs, years of cigarette smoking sawed at my chest in the rarefied air. My age hung on me like a heavy knapsack. Though it was usually below zero, my ice-encased underwear was slippery with sweat. It was a disgrace for a gym devotee like myself carrying nothing more than a sketchbook when I crashed into a ditch I was attempting to leap, while pack-and-rifle-carrying soldiers took it like ballet dancers. I realized then that war is for the very young. To carry bedroll, rations and rifle over six miles of uphill terrain with nothing at the end of it but a cold hole to sit in requires the resiliency and iron-muscle legs of a twenty-year-old.

On the tops of ice-coated mountains I huddled with shivering GI's, interviewing and sketching them. They sat in holes they had chopped from frozen ground. The snow-covered blankets and parkas pulled about them gave them the appearance of snowmen. They were hardly distinguishable from the icy hummocks that surrounded them. They were motionless. Plumes of breath hung about them. Frozen hands were jammed into armpits. They wore icy spike-like beards. Their faces were seamed like road maps.

One of them cracked wryly, "Us snowmen make swell photographs for the picture magazines. Can't you see me on the cover of *Life*," as he draped his blanket, grandmother style, about his face.

No matter how forlorn their circumstance, there was GI humor wherever I went. The frozen topography of twin mountain crests inspired the tag of "Jane Russell peaks."

Every bit of gear, food and ammunition was carried on soldier backs from valley CP's to the observation posts. A sergeant, toiling up a steep slope under a load of ammunition with sweat rolling down his face though it was then below zero, said, "They ought to send us some of those Missouri mules to pack this stuff. They'd be a Godsend." Another remarked, "Mexico belongs to the UN, doesn't it? If they can't send soldiers, why don't they ship us a couple of thousand burros? They'd save our aching backs."

One outpost squad I visited had the unwilling assistance of a cow in helping them to bring

up rations. The transport worked until "Elsie" plunged off the trail and down the mountainside with a week's rations on her back and the squad in hot pursuit. Private Tom Harris of Dawson Springs, Ky., said "Had to give her a burst so we could save the rations." His "How would you like some barbecued beef?" dramatized the fate of Elsie.

One day I came upon a corporal standing guard over a private who was slowly eating C-ration hash. He jabbed unenthusiastically at the can. Several empties lay at his feet. The corporal referred to the reluctant diner as "Trigger happy."

"Trigger here took a shot at me when I was bringing up rations last night. The bullet creased my collar and went right through the box. I'm making him eat every damn one he punctured."

Trigger's explanation of "enemy movement in the dark" failed to move the implacable corporal. When I said goodbye, Trigger was starting his sixth can.

Life in the valleys behind the forward positions was not so unhappy. At a Buddhist-temple company headquarters, 250-pound Ralph Giles of Pittsburgh, Pa., stood on the steps giving a powerful rendition of the drinking song from *The Student Prince* when I arrived. It was but one of the twenty complete scores of light operas he had learned. When not singing, the round-faced boy—he looked like Robert Morley, the British actor—was company runner. He didn't mind the job; in fact it had slimmed him down twenty-five pounds.

"If I get it down far enough, they'll give me romantic light opera leads when I get back."

I stopped for coffee one day with Captain Michael Cariglia, chaplain from Worcester, Mass. The Catholic padre boasted of the honesty of his unit's enlisted men. One afternoon he had hung a freshly washed combat jacket on a tree to dry. When evening came, it had disappeared. The padre strode into the mess hall and announced that "some stinker" had stolen his jacket, and that it had better be hanging on the tree by next morning's reveille. In the morning, the tree's branches held an even half-dozen jackets.

In my first month along the static winter front I talked to hundreds of soldiers and officers.

It didn't take long for me to realize that the American Army I was seeing here in Korea was an altogether different body of men from the civilian Army I campaigned with across France and Germany in World War II.

Nearly all of these men had volunteered. They were young. Most were under twenty. I met several who confessed to sixteen and seventeen. They had exaggerated their ages to enlist. Twelve of the first twenty men I talked with hailed from sub-standard areas in three Southern states. The soldiers in France and Germany were deeply concerned with news of home. These men were not. My conversational gambits of "Do you think Joe Louis can make a comeback?" and "Why did the Dodgers collapse?" brought blank stares. In the other war, my "Do you have a job waiting for you?" or "Are you getting married?" released a flow of excited words. They were wasted on the young soldiers I met here.

None of them had ever worked at a job. They had come into the Army directly from high school. They had never known American girls. The only girls they knew were the Terukos and Mitzios they had met while on occupation duty in Japan. The word "home" awakened little nostalgia. These men had "found a home in the Army." Their other home was Japan. The colonel of the regiment that reached the Yalu first told me that "Welcome home" banners, anticipating the regiment's return, had been strung above the streets of the Japanese town where they had been stationed in occupation duty. The same colonel described the men of the army in Korea as a beginning of a "true professional Army, America's Foreign Legion." He described them as "the lost generation of World War II."

"Father's in the Army, Mother's in defense work. They were neglected—they envied the men in uniform. They enlisted at the first opportunity. They may be considered bad boys back home but they're good boys here. While the civilian at war thinks always of home, the future of these men is here, with the regiment. The squad is his family and the sergeant is his father."

In the main I found that what he said was true. However, the draftees who were beginning to trickle into Korea reminded me of the World War II civilian soldiers.

The noncommissioned officers were older, almost middle-aged, fat-and-forty sergeants who had reenlisted.

This was a tougher war for the soldiers than the European conflict. It wasn't pleasant in the ETO—no war ever is—but there were compensations that helped keep soldier morale high. From the day of the Saint-Lô victory, the end of the war had been in sight. Here, the men on the front could see nothing but hundreds of rows of Heartbreak Ridges ahead of them with only a dubious peace in prospect. To the men who came here, Korea was only a name on a map, while to the soldiers of the other war, Europe was part of their lives. Their heritage was based on European culture. Nearly every boy had read *King Arthur* or *The Three Musketeers*. He knew about the Eiffel Tower and Heidelberg, had heard the music of the famous French and German composers, while the culture of the East meant absolutely nothing to him. The men in Korea were not hailed as liberators. There were no flowers pelting them or pretty girls throwing kisses. Korea was a poor country without clean houses to warm themselves in, or exciting cities with sidewalk cafés and shows. There was none of the loot of Europe to take home, no Rolliflexes, Lugers, cuckoo clocks or meerschaum pipes. There was nothing here to take as a souvenir but a high-crowned black straw hat, a Russian potato masher, a Mao Tse-tung poster or, if one were extraordinarily lucky, an enemy bugle.

Morale was low when I arrived in January, 1951. The headlong retreats from the Chinese border and the "Little Big Horn" action had discouraged the soldiers. The first question I was usually asked was "When are we getting out?" To them, the war was hopeless and lost. When the war had begun, occupation units were sent in from Japan to throw back an underestimated enemy. Our troops had been softened by easy occupation duty that saw no maneuvers. None of the men

I talked to had ever been trained under live ammunition before they had come here. The entry of the Chinese with their overwhelming man power had flattened their confidence in themselves. They wanted out.

They weren't green any more. They were battle-hardened. All they lacked at this period was confidence. The Ridgway appointment three months later proved to be the shot in the arm which they needed. The new battle tactics of keeping the line of advance unbroken protected the flanks. There were no more of the late General Walker's precipitant Patton-like sweeps around the ends in which Chinese pouring from enemy-held hills massacred cut-off units.

Soldiers always gripe and the Americans in Korea were no exception. Their gripes were not directed at the home front, as in the other war, but were aimed at "chicken" behind the front, at General Almond's headquarters where white-helmeted, kerchiefed honor guards paraded and combat men were employed shining staff cars and shoveling two hundred truckloads of sand to make a nice parade ground. There was almost actual hate against the Tokyo "commandos"—the "fat cats" who worked a five-day week directing traffic and running PX's, and drank real beer and chased real girls.

For a soldier sitting on a frozen Korean peak, life was immediate and very real. Most of his time was spent in an effort to keep alive against a fanatic enemy and Arctic cold. He knew only what his red-rimmed eyes saw and what his half-frozen ears heard. He had experienced seven months of all-out war and none of it had been good. Before him stretched endless rows of Korea's east-to-west mountain ranges, every one of them held by an enemy that barked fire until dead. He was alone except for the man on either side of him. VK, if it ever came, would not set off the hysterical VE- and VJ-day celebrations of six years before on Main and Broadway. Back home they were tired of Korea and would slam shut the covers on the book and proceed to forget it— and him.

These were the thoughts that drove the American soldier in Korea closer to his GI comrades —and farther from the world outside.

Sgt. W. Van der Sman
of Denhaag

Sgt. L. M. Beelhood
of Toronto

Dutch Heavy Weapons
Sketched near
the Han River
Korea

3 · Wooden Shoes and Turbans

The British played football, the Dutch smoked meerschaums, the Indians drank tea and the French hunted rabbits during the lull on the winter front.

The Dutch serenaded us with *Show Me The Way To Go Home* in perfectly enunciated English, accompanied by a harmonica and a guitar, as we approached. The wiry blond men were a far cry from the plump burghers pictured in Rembrandt's *Night Watch*. The high-spirited troopers invited sniper fire as they ridge-walked and larked in plain sight of the enemy-held village in the valley below their position.

The athletic men shed their parkas. It was a sunny day and quite warm. They strode about in underwear tops, aired blankets and sleeping bags. It was hard to realize that they had been through weeks of tough warfare. While waiting for a renewal of the shooting war, copy-hungry correspondents in search of "color" stories had been visiting the Dutch daily. To provide Netherlands atmosphere for visiting journalists, the sophisticated soldiers had worked out a routine. Today's performance began with my arrival.

A soldier in "Dutch boy" cap, meerschaum pipe and wooden shoes offered us Edam cheese wedges. Two boys figure-skated on their "canals." The others sang Dutch songs and stamped their feet. A lieutenant waved his arms suggestive of windmill sails. The correspondents, given their "color," the Hollanders sang *Lili Marlene* and *Swanee River* to guitar accompaniment.

Spike-bearded Sergeant Van Der Sman of Denhaag told me how the guitar had been secured on "Operation Guitar" the night before.

A reconnoitering patrol had entered the village below and set it afire. As they were retiring to their own lines, they missed a corporal. A few moments later, they heard shooting and could see him in the line of the burning buildings. He was running in the midst of rifle fire, one arm bloody, the other waving his guitar trophy. They covered his precipitant retreat. Before being evacuated this morning, the corporal exacted a promise from the platoon that they would guard the guitar until he returned with his arm repaired. In the meantime, eager Segovias fought for turns at it.

Dutch headquarters was really a bit of Holland transplanted. It was a tiny hamlet of high-gabled houses, romantically set in a valley of fir trees. Wooden bridges arched over a frozen canal on which soldiers off duty skated. The red, white and pale blue bars of the Dutch flag splashed color against the green of trees.

Outside the Dutch kitchen, mess orderlies milked a cow and churned butter. Inside, Mess Sergeant Jan Van Den Berg of Amsterdam baked biscuits of Pillsbury flour. Private Henricus Von Bruekelen of Utrecht roasted chickens raised in Wahoo, Neb. Von Bruekelen kiddingly asked me how the Dodgers were doing.

They sent us on our way with pockets full of biscuits and drumsticks.

For the past week, world headlines had featured a now-legendary French bayonet charge. There were stories of maddened Frenchmen spontaneously charging with cold steel, their blades dripping with gore, with terrified North Koreans fleeing before them. They had been compared with Napoleon's invincible guards.

Columns of correspondents jeeped daily to their bivouac south of the Han. While eager to interview and sketch the heroes, visions of beef ragout sped me in their direction. I anticipated an exciting change from press-camp C rations.

I had to abandon the jeep and hike over a roadless Bruegelesque winter landscape of rolling snow-covered hills and wandering paths, leafless poplar trees crowned with storks' nests and thatched-roof villages. A solitary crow spiraled in the clear blue sky. I dropped to the shelter of a snowbank at the crack of a rifle. Guerrillas! Another shot made me huddle even deeper in the snow.

There was silence. Finally, I looked over the bank to see that my imagined assailant was but a rabbit hunter, his cartridge belt draped with the furry game. He offered me one, grinning broadly. He guided me to the French camp. There I saw a piratical-looking crew in turtleneck sweaters, berets, untied pile caps, deer flaps pointing in every direction, their boottops unlaced. There were beards of every known style from Bluebeard to Monty Woolley. Some wore bright red parachute-silk scarves wrapped around their heads, buccaneer style. One sported a cushion-size Chinese fur hat to which he had attached a fox tail.

Most of them were sharpening bayonets and testing them on hairs pulled from their beards. They must have been warned of a correspondent on the horizon. I picked picturesque-looking Corporal Mathieu Daniel, ex-Normandy farmer, for my first model. While he whetted a twelve-inch blade, his comrades ringed us, volunteering the usual sidewalk-critic art comments. When I asked for a bayonet-charge story, hawk-nosed Private Alfred Lanet of Dijon, hero of the attack, was pushed forward.

To tell his story better, he fixed his bayonet to his rifle, and accompanied his description with unabashed eagerness. With fierce gestures and cat-like grins as the blade sank home, he said:

"We French relieved a platoon that was attacked by more than six hundred enemy. As we got into position, the Koreans came at us. Some of them were wearing American and Russian uniforms. They fired tommy guns from the waist. When our lieutenant gave the command, we charged. Another private and I ran so fast that we found ourselves way out in front. I fired from the hip until my magazine was empty. I went with my bayonet at the first fellow like this. He was pointing his gun at me. He was big, had a star on his cap. I lunged at his groin. I could see his face about to scream. My bayonet hit his belt and didn't give and didn't go in. I knocked him down with my rifle butt. I stuck him twice to make sure. I had to put my foot on his chest to get my rifle out. A *Rouge Koréen* on my right was firing at me. I went after him. Like that," he snapped his fingers, "I had him. Another one in baggy pants ran away. I chased him and caught him in the back."

His graphic account excited the others—they were taking out their press clippings—they all wanted to re-enact the attack. They fixed bayonets and mock-charged all about me, shouting and cursing as they stabbed. I still have a slit in the tail of my trench coat. Guerrillas hiding in the hills behind us must have shivered.

"—he was twisting so stuck him twice to make sure!"

25

An orderly extended a luncheon invitation from the French commander Lieutenant Colonel Monclar. I followed him happily to headquarters. The beef ragout at the officers' mess should be good.

He received me in a tiny Korean hut. The fifty-four-year-old Colonel, who was really General Ralph Magrim-Vernerey, had taken a reduction in rank to enable him to command the small French expeditionary force. The "Monclar" was a pseudonym he had assumed to protect his family while fighting with the Free French Army in World War II. He was a veteran of thirty-six years of war, from World War I to the fighting in Indo-China. He looked strikingly like Sir Cedric Hardwicke. He had the same mature charm. He insisted I help him lower the contents of a canteen filled with rum. The room was hot from the stoked floor. The addition of rum practically melted me. The Colonel was cool, though he wore a heavy woolen British tunic. He laughed when I mentioned the bayonet charge, saying that his troops would wear themselves out with their strenuous re-enactments of it for visiting reporters.

"My excited boys never had a chance to use their bayonets in Indo-China, but here the fanatical enemy attacks present targets. The Communists dig in deeply. Sometimes the only way to root them out is with the bayonet."

He criticized UN tactics. He attributed our defeats to our policy of keeping to the valleys.

"The army that holds the high ground can always dominate the valleys. There is only one way to fight guerrillas and that is to go into the hills after them and not advance until all of them are wiped out. We are an army on wheels. Our tanks and heavy equipment tie us to the roads."

While he talked, I sketched. The drawing and rum were finished at the same time and we went next door to lunch. We were served cold C rations still in the can! This, in French headquarters' mess! France had sent its best soldiers to Korea, but not its best cooks.

When I arrived back at press camp, Warren White showed me a wishbone he was saving.

"There was chicken for lunch," he told me. "First time this winter."

The Argyles scored a goal against the Middlesex team in the football game they were playing as I arrived at British brigade headquarters.

Husky soldiers dribbled, kicked and bounced the ball with their heads while off-duty comrades cheered and puzzled Korean villagers stared. Argyle heads were covered with jaunty Balmoral tams and Middlesex heads with scarves twisted into stocking caps.

In the afternoon sun, soldiers played with round-faced children and romped with furry puppies that looked like miniature bears. Soldier laundry dried stiffly on clothes lines. The villagers worked at farm tasks, carrying water, stacking hay and feeding stock. Somewhere a bagpipe was skirling. In a Nativity-like tableau, cows and sheep munched hay in an open shed. The great brown eyes of the oxen reflected the active pastoral scene about them. An arm-swinging Signal platoon, their backs loaded with equipment, drilled in a farm courtyard. I sketched their captain, Nigel Crow of York. His handsome head was lost in an inch-thick wool turtleneck sweater. He wore elbow mittens.

An apple-cheeked Middlesex private asked me to photograph him, standing next to his jeep. He wanted a picture to send his girls—both of them, Sibyl and Mary. Their names graced the windshield of the jeep. To free my arms, I laid my musette bag on the jeep's hood. This photo-taking started a run. Privates Ray Field and Stan Thompson wanted me to snap them together. Both were nineteen, were mortar men and had lived across the street from each other in Chertsey all their lives.

When I reached for my musette, I found it was gone with the jeep. The bag contained a month's work—notes, sketches, film—which I carried with me for safety's sake.

Captain Crow's platoon scattered in every direction to search for it. The football game stopped and players and spectators joined in the hunt. Within an hour, an area a mile in every direction was explored without success. My only hope was that the bag might still be on the hood of the jeep when the vehicle returned to camp.

The jeep drove into camp, minus the musette bag. The apple-cheeked driver said he had not seen it. He had been to another village several miles down the road. My only hope now was to follow the jeep's route.

I set out on what I was certain would be a hopeless search. I stopped every vehicle. No luck. About midway between the two villages, I sighted a familiar shape in a snowbank. I broke into a trot, picked it up, pulled back the flap. The precious-to-me sketches and notebooks were there, as well as the film cans. They were crushed but legible. My snow goggles had been smashed. A vehicle must have passed over them. Whoever had picked up the bag had taken my wool muffler, mittens and chocolate bar, which he probably needed more than I. Anyway, I was happy to have the sketches back. For once in my life a negative appraisal of my art overjoyed me!

Dinner at brigade headquarters was the usual meagre fare of a British mess. The scant portions of bully beef disappeared quickly and hungry officers allayed their appetites with endless cups of tea and piles of soda crackers. They listened attentively while they ate to news items from a bundle of freshly-arrived month-old London papers read by a monocled brigadier.

I was bedded comfortably for the night on a heated hut floor with an engineer officer and the brigade's PRO and chaplain. Their natural reserve was melted by the bottle of whiskey I produced from my trenchcoat pocket. So friendly was our sleeping-bag acquaintance that the engineer promised me a share in his inheritance, a pub in Sussex, The Horse and Goat.

Our peaceful predawn sleep was shattered by flame and bullet explosions. I heard shouts of "Guerrillas!" and "Attack!" We poured out of the door in panic. When we got outside, we realized that our hut was afire. The overhot oven had ignited the floor and burning ammunition belts were responsible for the "shooting."

While we shoveled snow on the house, the chaplain gallantly risked life and limb when he dashed into the hut amidst flame and popping ammunition to rescue the precious whiskey bottle. The only casualties of the fire were our sleeping bags.

A lorry-type ambulance turned into the road ahead of us on the return trip to Second Division

headquarters. I caught a glimpse of its driver. He was wearing a turban. I was anxious to see the Indian Ambulance Corps so I followed the lorry over a bouncy stretch of corduroy road into the courtyard of a Korean schoolhouse.

A squad of helmeted soldiers, thin and dark-faced, trotted smartly to the lorry and unloaded a groaning casualty. I talked to the driver, Karim Singh of Punjab. The six-foot bearded Indian held himself very erect as he answered my questions in perfect English. He was a paratrooper. Had action in Kashmir to his credit. Liked everything about Americans, especially their mechanized equipment. He confessed to an ambition to drive one of our two-and-a-half-ton trucks.

To my question, "Do you like Korean girls?" Singh answered, "No." He saluted splendidly as Captain Dass, very tiny beside the Sikh, invited me inside for tea.

Large-eyed, handsome, sensitive-faced officer doctors were ringed around a potbellied stove. Scotch as well as tea was being served. The officers wore British uniforms and their long pointed mustaches were of English type. All the doctors were paratroopers and were veterans of Burma and Kashmir.

Sepoy Karim Singh of Punjab Ambulance Driver

Talking with them, I learned that the Indian Ambulance Corps was one of the few UN units in Korea that was not supplied and equipped by the United States. The transport that had brought the corps from India had also carried their ambulances, operating tables, medical supplies and, in addition, a year's food supply—rice ("None of the Korean night-soil variety for us!") and typically Indian foods like *dhall, atta,* and *ghee,* as well as condiments for their beloved curries. However, fresh meat was furnished them from American supplies.

Religious food taboos did not exist here. Mohammedans, Sikhs, and Hindus had put aside their dietary differences for the duration.

The doctors were eager for me to see them at work. I watched Captains Dass and Rangaswami of Madras operate on a Korean boy brought in a few minutes before, his arm shattered by a hand grenade he had been playing with. Captain J. M. Rau of Naisannapet demonstrated his painless dentistry as he filled the teeth of a Middlesex corporal. His drill was powered by a foot pedal. Within an hour he filled the corporal's teeth, wired a New Zealander's broken jaw and cleaned a brigadier's teeth.

Captain Asoke Banerjee of Bihar, assisted by a handsomely-bearded Sikh, Sanjan Singh of Jumma, administered blood plasma to a wounded British boy.

The sound of bebop guided me to the enlisted men's barracks, where I saw a dozen Moslems, Hindus, Sikhs and Gurkhas clapping hands in democratic harmony as they crouched around a record player. The turbans of some of the less inhibited Sikhs had unfurled, exposing their uncut hair, which was caught into buns. The record collection had originally been Indian. Grateful American patients had presented the corps with a stack of bebop and jazz records.

I felt it was incongruous to hear turbaned Sikhs enthusiastically discussing boogie woogie in a house in the mountains of Central Korea. These Indian Ambulance corpsmen who carry rifles as well as stretchers are legendary for their bravery under fire. They have never been known to abandon a stretcher, even under heavy attack. An American officer once told me, "If I'm ever hit, I hope the Indians pick me up."

This was deserved tribute.

I rejoined the officer-doctors for a final whiskey and soda around the stove. As we talked, I became more and more aware of how British they really were. I might have been in a London club during the last war. Copies of *Punch* and *Sketch*—teatime—the batmen—the British uniforms and mustaches—the clipped Oxford accents all demonstrated an admiration of things British. I remembered the ill feeling that existed between the Indians and the British and I wondered how the Ambulance Corps felt about being attached to the British Brigade. Did they mind?

Over a whiskey and soda, Dass replied, "Decidedly not—after all, we belong to the same club."

4 • Figures in a Fiery Landscape

Central Korea was aflame and the roads were filled with its dispossessed the morning Warren White and I jeeped to Cheechon. In a scene that might have been lifted from a Hieronymus Bosch landscape, burning villages spouted flame and columns of smoke joined a skywide pall that hid the sun. The fleeing inhabitants streamed over roads and paths leading to the south past barren trees that lifted their stunted arms as though in angry indictment.

We were witnessing the UN armies' scorched-earth policy in action. The torch of "military necessity" had been put to farms and villages to destroy them and to prevent their use as shelter by an infiltrating enemy. Unfortunately, this meant that their warmth and comfort was also denied to their innocent owners.

The refugees trudged hopelessly, looking back now and then at their fiery homes. Many of them, though they had come a short distance, were already tired by their heavy burdens of household belongings. Old men gasped for breath as they rested their towering "A"-frame loads on road-banks. The children wore tiny knapsacks. Some mothers with bale-size bundles balanced on their heads used their free arms to hug freezing babies to icy breasts. There were stretches of the road restricted to military traffic. Here they were forced to detour. Ribbons of white-clad figures followed paths that wound over fir-dotted slopes. Bridges were off limits to them. They crossed on the ice.

It was at least twenty miles to the towns that lay beyond the rim of the burning sector. Freezing night would catch the pitiful columns in the mountains. Without shelter, some would certainly die.

We were tempted to carry some of the old people in our jeep but MP's at the first crossroad would have forced us to dump them. Whenever we slowed the jeep, girls offered themselves to us in payment for rides for exhausted parents.

When we stopped for lunch, hungry children gathered to watch us as we opened our "C's." We tossed them the cans and drove on.

Cheechon, once a good-sized prosperous town on the main railroad, now was broken and burned. The tracks of the prosperity-bringing railroad had guided American bombers to it like arrows. Bored American GI's, hating Korea, friend and foe alike, had completed its ruin. Window panes had been smashed. Dresser drawers had been dumped on floors, their contents scattered. Toys and pencil sets and inkwells and earthenware pots had been swept from shop shelves into the streets. Our feet crunched them as we walked. Barber chairs had been ripped from their moorings and now served as seats for traffic-directing MP's. Dead horses and sheep swelled on sidewalks. Trucks and tanks had gouged the streets to a mire. Signal-company men had strung wire from every remaining vertical wall and pole. A Buddhist statue on the town's edge served as a telephone pole. Wire streamed from it in every direction. I had sketched a crucified Christ at a St. Mère Église intersection back in Normandy. It, too, had been draped with wire like this statue.

The sixty miles of front stretching from Cheechon to the Japan Sea on Korea's east was loosely held. ROK—Republic of Korea—units defending this line were widely separated and unable to prevent infiltration of enemy troops. Cheechon formed the anchor of a firmly held front extending from the west. The Seventh Division which held Cheechon was in the process of linking

Roles checking ot Cranwon

up with the ROK's. A strong patrol had pushed as far as Yongwol, a third of the way to the coast. The road between the two towns, Yongwol and Cheechon, was lightly held. Guerrillas ambushed small patrols and mined the road. During the day the road was mineswept and jeeps were convoyed by tanks. At night the road was closed to military traffic. Between dark and dawn it became a no man's land.

After we left the barbed wire of Cheechon's outer perimeter, the road paralleled the railroad embankment. Sabotaging guerrillas had torn up its rails. At times the upended ties and rails looked like picket fences.

We slowed the jeep to talk to ROK men and women soldiers guarding a road block. They were searching refugee bundles. Innocent looking bundles of clothes sometimes hold mortar shells and machine-gun ammunition. Soldiers were thorough in their search. They probed baskets of rice with their bayonets.

The short, stocky soldiers of South Korea enjoyed an undeserved reputation as inferior fighting men among other UN troops. The "gooks," as they were called scornfully by GI's, had yielded disastrously many times to the ferocious attacks of their northern brethren, but they were generally ill-equipped, badly led and without tank and artillery support. Now they were being retrained, better equipped and given artillery support. With their improved condition, their morale was high and they were giving a good account of themselves in battle. The "gook" appellation was now an almost fond one.

These guards were typical of the new Korean army. Privates Chung-tai-wun of Seoul and Shingen-ka of Yonchon had been issued weapons but no GI uniforms as yet. They were eager for uniforms because in their peasant dress they could be mistaken for enemy partisans, especially at night. One of their comrades had been killed a few days before by an American sentry with a nervous trigger finger.

The two moonfaced ROK girl soldiers had been issued their uniforms and filled them out plumply. They were serious soldiers who were not as quick to smile as other Orientals. The shorter of the ROK girls was nearly as husky as a Minnesota fullback. Her wide face and ample breasts that bulged out her GI field jacket reminded me of a Russian WAC I had seen directing traffic in Berlin.

A half mile beyond the ROK's, engineers, using dynamite in an effort to pry loose a $75,000 Pershing tank that was mired in the mud of a bypass, warned us to take cover. We sheltered ourselves from exploding mud and rocks in a snow-filled draw. I tripped over the legs of a dead North Korean soldier. His lifeless hands were locked about the branches of a dwarf pine as though in death he was impelled to hold something green and living. The oyster white of his quilted uniform barely outlined him in the dirty snow. Blood from a terrible wound in his neck had dried into purple epaulets. The body was odorless. The smell of death would come with the spring thaws.

White was busy photographing a body a few yards away. He turned to me and yelled, "This should be a good shot: 1/100th of a second at 5.6." I looked at his subject. The skull had been scooped out by a shell fragment, giving a grisly effect. Another corpse, propped on a bank, crouched like a gargoyle. Its frozen grin held a cigarette from a macabre GI's pack.

When the dynamiting was over, we left quickly. A convoy of speeding jeeps careened past us and were lost to sight as they rounded a curve. We heard a clap like thunder and saw a figure sail over the hill pursued by smoke and flame, his legs churning the air like a cyclist. When we arrived at the scene a half moment later, the crumpled ruin of a smoking jeep told us what had happened. A crowd of soldiers surrounded its unharmed survivor, Corporal Raymond Lunny of Philadelphia, Pa., who had been blown fifty feet into the air and was alive to tell about it.

"My jeep was last in the column. Suddenly it blew three ways and I went up in the air like I was tossed by a broncho. I thought I'd never come down. I felt like the guy on the flying trapeze. I landed in the snow running, and I kept running 'cause I thought it was artillery. I didn't stop until I heard the guys yelling. Boy! Am I glad it's winter and there was snow to fall in! I'll never kick about Korea weather again."

As his astonishing escape from death dawned more fully on him, Lunny added: "Nothing like this ever happened to me at Blumenthal's chocolate factory."

This was dramatic proof that even well-traveled, mineswept roads were unsafe. We drove slowly, watching for telltale fresh dirt patches, and kept well away from the road's shoulders.

Along about midafternoon, we came to what was left of a dynamited bridge. It was impossible to proceed further. The land on the other side of the river was, for the most part, held by the enemy, except for the American patrol in Yongwol, seven miles distant.

An air attack on the enemy across the river was just beginning. An enemy patrol in company strength had been spotted near the railroad, we were told by an artillery officer who came up as we watched. We could see Marine Corsairs circling and diving beyond the first row of snowy ridges across from us. They dropped cylinders of napalm. Heavy black columns of smoke curled skyward. Later, we were told that the North Koreans had sheltered themselves from the bombs in a railroad tunnel. Bombs sealed shut both ends of the tunnel, burying them alive. A cluster of prisoners, herded by American infantrymen, forded the river and mounted the bank near us, among them an old man and two teen-age boys in peasant clothing.

I followed the prisoners into a farm courtyard that served as a PW cage. The old man and the boys were put into a low-ceilinged room. The boys had been caught carrying grenades in their bundles and the old peasant had been found climbing through a barbed wire entanglement. He continued to protest that he had lost his way while trying to bring rice to his wife inside Yongwol Refugees from his village had told him she was there and was starving.

Prisoners captured after a battle always look beaten and bedraggled but the North Korean soldiers I saw in the farmyard were an especially mournful-looking group. Gobs of dirty cotton hung from rents in their quilted coats. Their bare feet were purple and swollen to football size from frostbite. There was little of the legendary defiance and arrogance of North Koreans taken in the early fighting of the war. The winter war had been even worse for them than for the American snowmen. American planes had smashed their supply lines. Their uniforms and shoes had worn out. There had been little food, only a bowl of rice daily, barely enough to keep alive on. The freezing soldiers had been unable to build fires to warm themselves—fire brought American planes. Unrelenting hardship, bombs and napalm had shattered their morale. This group had given itself up.

Private Shin-Kun Ho, twenty-two-year-old farmer from Nae-nam-myon, typified these prisoners. While he chopsticked voraciously through bowls of rice, he talked without reservation to his interrogators. The Communists had forced him into the army and after a short training period, which was mostly indoctrination, he had been marched with the men from his village—they were all dead now—to the front. All of the marching had been at night. They had hidden by day from American planes. No food had been issued them. They were told to scrounge from the country-side, but there was nothing to eat in the empty farmhouses along their route. He had been hungry all of the time, and frozen. He and his comrades were discouraged. Easy victory had been promised them but they soon saw that rifles were no match for bombs and napalm. His squad had been on patrol. When they saw American soldiers, they surrendered to them.

It was late afternoon when we started on the return trip. The road was deserted. We saw no one. We made one stop. White was hankering for a souvenir. He wanted one of the black, high-crowned straw hats that distinguished Korean patriarchs. He thought he might find one in one of the deserted farmhouses.

As White and I walked up to a small house, we heard muted sobbing through a torn rice-paper window. As we slid open the door, the sobbing stopped.

A small figure lay on a bed of rags in a dark corner of the room. It was a boy, half-naked and shuddering. The right side of his face was swollen to pumpkin size. A yellowish pus coursed over his cheek from nose, mouth and eyes. Near the bed was a rusty helmet, half filled with uncooked rice grains.

He looked at us fearfully as we approached him. We must have loomed frighteningly large in that small room. I could see that he was holding his lips tight in a desperate effort not to cry. To show him we were friendly, I put a piece of chocolate on his chest. When he saw we meant no harm, he began to whimper. It was evident to us that he had been deserted because he was too sick to travel. It was a moment of agonizing decision. White and I were afraid if we attempted to move him he might die. Yet, he would surely die if we left him—we could not come back. So we poured water from our canteens into a bottle, opened a can of stew and placed it with crackers on the floor next to his bed where he could reach them. There was nothing more we could do for him. We left silently.

Twilight was deepening as we passed the mired tank which the engineers had finally aban-doned. Two white-clad figures leaped down from the turret, dragging a tank ammunition belt with them. They disappeared into the darkness under the bridge.

The quick close view of the enemy panicked us. White's foot jammed the gas pedal flush with the floor. Moments later we were warming ourselves at a friendly bonfire within Cheechon's outer perimeter.

5·An American in Tokyo

The sun-bathed Tokyo that greeted my eyes on my return wiped away my original dreary impression.

Along the Ginza—Tokyo's Fifth Avenue—tiny almond-eyed women who might have stepped from old Japanese prints clattered by on wooden clogs, their bright orange and red flowered kimonos splashing gaily against the background of soldier khaki. They tilted forward as they walked to support the baby bundles on their backs. *Furoshiki*—brightly colored silk scarves—were their shopping bags.

Towering Americans and Australians shouldered like Gullivers above the miniature Japanese. Some of the soldiers escorted pudding-faced girls wearing heavy mascara and large painted mouths. Short skirts swirled over their bowling pin legs. Farm women in drooping blue pantaloons gaped at window displays of electrical appliances—irons, toasters, washers. Workmen cycled past, wearing parts of old uniforms and smocks emblazoned with beer ads. One of them carried a heavy iron radiator on his back. American wives and their gum-popping offspring, mother in mink, children in pigtails, levis and checkered shirts worn outside, marched with the proud assurance of conquerors. Schoolboys in dark-blue, buttoned-to-the-throat uniforms and black-visored caps, but wearing no sox, raced through the crowd. American sailors and Russian officers from the Soviet Embassy eyed each other as they shopped under the awnings of curb stalls.

In the center of the city, the medieval lines of the Palace were sharpened by the clear sky above. In the moat below the Palace walls, ducks paddled and carp raced for crumbs tossed by children. Across the street from the Palace, a crowd waited in front of the Dai-Ichi Building. The daily gallery of Japanese and American soldier-sightseers pushed forward and snapped pictures as General Douglas MacArthur, followed by a retinue of high brass, strode from door to waiting car, his head high and his jaw set as he received his kingly due of clicking heels and smart salutes. I saw the unvarying pomp and circumstance of his entries and exits many times in the days that followed. There was always a huge crowd and they loved every awesome moment.

I was billeted—luckily for me, in overcrowded Tokyo—at the Correspondents' Club on narrow Shimbun ("Newspaper") Alley. On my arrival, I found most of the war reporters in the Club's bar. The only girl present was Marguerite Higgins, freshly returned from a Hong Kong-Formosa visit. She wore an eye-filling Chinese silk gown that fitted like a sheath. The slit skirt displayed her shapely legs to the knee. Little snub-nosed Bob Vermillion of United Press embarrassed Maggie with his fulsome account of her rejection by Geisha girls at Mioshi's the evening before. A party of correspondents had taken her with them and introduced her to the girls as an American Geisha. The serious little Japanese professionals, not seeing the humor of the situation, had resented this foreign competition from a non-Tokyo Geisha Guild member. She had been forced to leave.

Tom Lambert of Time, Inc., Hal Boyle, UP, and Fred Sparks, *Chicago Daily News,* argued grand strategy over beer and Scotch with little Joe From, *U.S. News and World Report.* Romantically bearded British correspondents in berets graced one end of the bar. Conversation was interrupted frequently by Vermillion's quavering yodel of "Boooooy-saaan!" which brought hurrying Japanese bus boys and waiters.

The ever-busy bar is the Club's main source of income. The Club buys its liquor at Army prices, minus tax. Foreseeing the end of the Occupation, the provident Club management had bought all the whiskey the Club could hold. The cellar was filled and overflow boxes of the precious fluid were stacked ceiling-high, lining all the halls. Even the billiard table was piled with it, six tiers high.

Hungry reporters, just returned from Korea, packed the restaurant, eating shrimp, steak and frozen strawberries and grabbing at petite Japanese waitresses. After the solemn deadpan girls of Korea, the animated giggling countenances of the waitresses were most attractive to them. I made the comment at one of the tables that the face of the girl serving us, while attractive, bore a strong resemblance to that of Joe Louis. Her chief pursuer gasped, "Never thought I'd end up chasing girls who looked like Joe Louis!"

"Bivouac" was the proper description for the room to which I was assigned. In pre-Korea war days, two could live comfortably in it. Now there were beds for eight. The Club was overcrowded. Two hundred correspondents lived off and on in quarters designed for about twenty. Sometimes the overflow had to be accommodated in cots set up in the library and in the halls.

My room was further crowded with piles of luggage and clothing left behind by reporters now in Korea. Their shaving tools, fountain pens, wrist watches—sometimes passports, piles of money and weapons—lay scattered carelessly on tables and bureaus. In the six months I lived in and out of the Club, I never heard a single instance of an article disappearing. I always felt secure in leaving my camera and typewriter behind when I went on assignments. I knew they'd be on the table when I returned.

Sleeping was well-nigh impossible. When stories broke, the typewriters pounded all night. Amorous writers sometimes smuggled girls into their cots and distressingly disturbed the sleep of the girlless. Casualties from the bar were dumped into bed and snored stentoriously. Work, too, was impossible for an artist. There was never an undisturbed moment nor a time when there was enough clear table space on which to prop a drawing board.

Sunday mornings sleepy correspondents dragged themselves and their aching heads from their beds to join the mass of soldiers and Occupation personnel converging on the Ginza PX.

The shelves at the PX are restocked on Sunday mornings and items in short supply and big demand, like cameras, portable radios and alarm-clock wrist watches, appear on the shelves. The eight floors in what was formerly a Japanese department store offer for sale everything from corsets to motor scooters. This Macy-like emporium anticipates the soldier's needs. He can buy cigarettes, candy, record players, souvenirs for the folks back home of Indian saris and kimonos. He can have his hair cut, his shoes repaired, or patches designed and sewn on his uniform. I designed a new shoulder patch for UN correspondents—a round blue patch with white lettering—which most correspondents use today.

For Occupation families, there are golf sticks, skis, girdles, baby foods, even a swap shop for the women.

Japanese teen-age sweater girls waited outside the PX doors daily for cigarette- and candy-laden GI's. They meet and spend the afternoon at the movies. The Japanese love Hollywood's action-packed thrillers.

The movies playing my first Sunday were all of them time-tested American classics: *Stage Coach, Northwest Passage, The Plainsman, One Million B. C.* and *The Unconquered.* There were several Japanese Westerns playing, featuring slit-eyed men in ten-gallon hats blazing away with six-shooters.

With nightfall, the love-hungry soldiers and their girls play amorously on the grass along the Palace moat. The soldiers without women drink beer in on-limits beer halls or read books at the Ernie Pyle Library.

I saw the tourist Tokyo quickly with sightseeing sailors and soldiers on temple and museum tours. With them, I watched the classic tea-pouring ceremonies and the Kabuki actors.

I saw the real Tokyo of work and pleasure with a Japanese friend, patient young Nioshi Keneko, an aviator turned businessman. He was generous of his time. We spent long hours exploring the great city.

The women and children of the working class of Tokyo especially delighted my artist's eye. The good-humored little women smiled and laughed squeakily at their simple jokes, as teams of them pulled heavy carts—sometimes with babies on their backs—or as they shopped for vegetables at the shoebox-size street stalls. They found life good. Their slanted eyes danced, rich blood damasked their wide healthy cheeks, and their robust mouths flashed pearly teeth. Sundays brought a chameleon-like change in their costume. They shed their dust- and mud-splattered blue coolie-cotton pantaloons and white aprons and appeared in bright cerise, purple and red kimonos. If it rained, they carried rainbow-colored parasols. Their hair was dressed in high coiffures and decorated with shell combs and flower pins. Their long working strides changed on Sunday to a dainty shuffling gait, caused by their kimono-wrapped knees, as they teetered past on high kiri-wood clogs.

The husky women were transformed by their costume and hairdress to graceful, delicate dolls.

The Japanese girls I saw in central Tokyo with bobbed hair and well ventilated knees had abandoned the traditional Japanese dress for the liberated look of the West, but had lost grace and beauty in the exchange.

The mothers were always surrounded by children—if a Japanese wife has but four children, she is considered ill. Japanese parents love their children less critically than any other parents I have ever seen. I never heard a cross word directed at a Japanese child. They fondle the children and play with them and buy them endless bags of colored bean candies, sugared peas and starch cakes, as well as Mickey Mouse balloons and toys. The beautifully quaint, puppy-like children populate every inch of the sidewalks of the outer city. Snub-nosed boys with hickory-nut shaved heads fight tops and bang shuttlecocks that whiz about the heads of passers-by. Once I saw an old beggar woman who had been using expertly wielded chopsticks to pick up cigarette butts along the curb catch one of the whizzing "birds" in mid-air with one quick movement of the chopsticks.

Little girls played with dolls—the baby sisters on their backs were no larger—and fed bits of cucumber to pet crickets in tiny cages made of silk thread.

The booming of the *Kami-Shibai's* (Story Teller's) drum attracts hordes of children. They pour from every doorway and alley. The Story Teller is to the Japanese child what comic books, radio, television and movies are to the American child. He mounts his miniature theatre on the handlebars of his bicycle. The *Kami-Shibai* slides crudely-drawn, vividly-colored picture cards into the theatre stage in sequence to illustrate the story he is telling. His listeners' almond eyes widen as they follow the story. They cheer and groan as heroes and villains gain advantage. Virtue always triumphs in these sidewalk dramas.

I joined the juvenile gallery several times. In one of the tales I saw and heard, the samurai hero wreaks tremendous vengeance on fire-breathing dragons and sword-wielding robber barons to gain a fair maiden, completely equipped with a dowry of lands and castle. Another show featured a slant-eyed Superman who, with the aid of his cape, flew into Fujiyama's cone to apprehend a nest of evildoers.

The excitement and color of Tokyo's street life compensated for the drab dullness of its buildings. Aside from the Palace and the temples, most of its architecture consisted of ugly adaptations of modern Western architecture. The "skyscrapers" of the central Maranouchi district were dirty gray cube-like structures resembling Leavenworth's prison blocks. Frank Lloyd Wright's famed Imperial Hotel was a great disappointment. To me, it seemed a squat, dark, ground-clinging, windowless mausoleum without the graceful beauty of the best of Oriental structures or the functional character of the West's best.

The rest of the city had the temporary boom-town appearance of any war-wrecked city under reconstruction with its long rows of flimsy unpainted jerry-built shacks.

Japanese shopkeepers consider it fashionable to advertise in English, much as American restaurants snobbishly print their menus in French. The combination of their native idiom and an unfamiliar language resulted in some startling announcements. Even Japanese Keneko laughed over a barber's "Head Cutting of Gentlemen," a tailor's "Fits Upstairs," and a furrier's "Ladies' Furs Made From Own Skins."

Keneko introduced me to his artist friends who in turn introduced me to other artists. Tokyo's "Left Bank" was completely Western. Bearded artists in berets, turtleneck sweaters and lumberjack shirts sat around *hibachis* (charcoal braziers) in cold-water studios, sipping tea and paying homage to the Paris masters. They had turned their backs on traditional Japanese painting and were complete devotees of Picasso, Matisse, Braque and Van Gogh. Many of the painters had slavishly imitated the styles and mannerisms of the Western masters they admired. In doing so, their Japanese subject matter looked anything but Japanese. A rainy Tokyo street scene looked like a rainy Paris street scene. A Japanese mountain landscape looked like the Alps or the Pyrenees. The only Japanese painters I know whose work really looks Japanese are Foujita in Paris and Kuniyoshi in New York.

At night central Tokyo is gay with lanterns and neon tubes exploding bright red, green and orange calligraphy, advertising restaurants and night clubs. *The Showboat's* neon-lighted paddles wheeled briskly over a canal. Keneko and I drank bad whiskey and watched endless slant-eyed chorus girls, corsages pinned on their twitching posteriors, in night clubs that were springing up like mushrooms. One club featured a nude lady charmer with snakes twining her breasts. Japanese businessmen have taken happily to night-club life. They drink whiskey—their tolerance is low—and fox-trot with evening-gowned hostesses—they don't bring their wives. They love the "high life" of the Western world.

We had eating as well as drinking adventures at night. We sat at *tempura* bars and ate shrimp, eel, octopus and lobster as fast as the cook behind the counter could fry them in a fluffy batter. We had many *sukiyaki* dinners but none as good as those I have experienced at the *Miyako* in New York. Late at night we bought fish snacks from gay-bannered pushcarts wheeled by coolies who piped on bamboo flutes and sang their menu.

A nocturnal ramble took us to Asakusa or "Lovey Town" as Keneko tabbed it. The half-mile-square area near the Asakusa R.R. station is completely devoted to joy. Thousands of charm-laden girls inhabit it. A billboard map at the "town's" entrance clearly charts the location of every pleasure establishment. Rickshaw pullers give gratuitous information and police information booths dot the area. The police were satisfied by my journalist's credentials which backed my reportorial business in this Coney Island of the libido. It is off limits to American soldiers. If it were on limits, the yen-hungry Momma-sans—Madams—would raise prices far beyond the capacity to pay off the pocket-poor Japanese men.

The girls sat in bars and parlors opening on to narrow, unpaved streets. The salons catered to all tastes. Some offered sultry sophisticated charmers in high heels and evening gowns; others, traditionally dressed girls in kimonos who touched knees and bowed as men inspected them. And there were bobby soxers in fuzzy sweaters and brown and white saddle oxfords. Through open windows, I could see girls painting their lips and faces from little ivory boxes and looking into postage-stamp-size mirrors as they prepared for their evening's work. The streets were filled with men who window-shopped or drank beer and *sake* at bars.

As night darkened, the girls withdrew to rear rooms and the streets emptied of men. Long rows of men's shoes appeared on door steps. I didn't carry my investigation of Asakusa further. Though I always attempt to be the empirical reporter, in this case my connubial obligation kept my shoes on my feet.

Keneko was unable to accompany me into "Occupation Tokyo." Signs barred Japanese from clubs, PX's, military buildings, reserved railroad cars, even some of the public washrooms. The men and women who had come from America to govern conquered Japan were, many of them, unfriendly to the Japanese. Alongside the mild-mannered Japanese, they seemed arrogant and thoughtless. They shouldered aside the Japanese on the street and were rude to them in the shops.

One day at a PX food counter, an Occupation housewife pushed the Japanese wife of an American serviceman to one side and shouted indignantly, "Since when are Orientals served while white people wait?"

Their children reflected their rude behavior. Boys in Hopalong-Cassidy boots and chaps snapped toy sixshooters in the surprised faces of Japanese men and women. Little girls ordered servants about and exacted dog-like obedience from them.

With the Occupation nearing its end, Army headquarters, foreseeing our need of future Japanese good will, issued a booklet for Occupation personnel. The booklet advised: "Don't be condescending. Treat your servants politely, treat them like people—don't shout at them"; "Choose your clothes for the time and place. Women, don't wear shorts and halters downtown in a metropolitan city like Tokyo"; "Mind your manners and behave yourself even if there are no military police around"; and "Remember that you may be sightseeing in Japan as a housewife but the Japanese will watch your actions as though you were an ambassador."

A correspondent on the eve of departure to Korea may go to bed early, but more likely he will join a party of fellow correspondents for a last visit to Mioshi's.

Stories I had heard of the Geisha houses which were off limits to soldiers but on limits to civilians had interested me. This time I was going along.

A reservation was made by phone and the names of Geisha favorites were given. We were met at the gates by Momma-san, an old Geisha with eyeglasses and a bevy of tittering white-

45

aproned maids. They escorted us to one of a half-dozen plywood houses dotted about a garden filled with dwarf pines, squat stone lanterns, bronze storks and goldfish pools.

The maids removed our shoes and we walked in our stockinged feet into a typical Japanese parlor with rice-paper walls, a decorative screen and a low table. We sat in our trench coats as the room was cold and drafty as is always the case in Japanese houses. We squatted on rice-straw mats, toasting our feet in the *Kotausu*—a concrete box filled with burning charcoal sunk in the floor under the table. While we waited for the Geisha to arrive, we drank whiskey from bottles we had brought with us and hot *sake* and Japanese beer served by the maids.

Suddenly from nowhere, Teruko, Novoko and Sogetu fluttered into the room, gliding over the floor to fall gracefully on their knees, arms crossed and heads bowed, at our sides. They were costumed in flowered silk kimonos, with brocaded *obi* (sashes). Their hair was ritually dressed in butterfly coiffures studded with mother-of-pearl and turquoise pins and combs. White, split-toed socks covered their tiny feet. They had the aristocratic oval faces seen in ancient Japanese prints. The petite olive-complexioned girls smiled demurely as they glanced up at tonight's lords and masters. We were overawed by their graceful female obeisance and willing to enact with them a romantic, dignified and ceremonious tableau. But Teruko broke the spell with the "Hiya, big boy" that came from her rosebud mouth as she slapped one of the correspondents on the back. It was going to be just an evening of girls after all.

These party girls had been spoiled by the American businessmen who were piling into Tokyo by the hundreds with plenty of money to spend. All through the evening, though the sensitive writers tried to keep them in their traditional role, they used American slang and songs in their effort to please.

Geisha girls begin their lives of entertainment at a tender age. A long schooling is given them to fit them for their combination role of hostess, mistress of ceremonies, singer, dancer and agreeable table companion. They are taught to play the *samisen* (a 17-string harp), serve *sake,* and flatter masculine vanity with polite conversation. When the training period ends, the girl is a full-fledged Geisha.

In the past, the Geisha belonged to the contractor who purchased her from her parents. Today, theoretically, she is a free agent but is still in debt and no more free than before. While a Geisha is supposed to get 50 per cent of the money she earns, actually most of her money is eaten up by living expenses, including a lavish wardrobe—Geishas have the same feminine love of clothes as their Western sisters. Geishas are eternally in debt and are hardly ever able to buy their "freedom." If a girl can't save enough to pay off the contractor, her only alternative is to marry a rich patron—if he is willing to divorce his wife. Though there is plenty of business, black-market operators with plenty of yen to spend and American businessmen—who find Geisha houses infinitely more interesting than Buddhist temples—there is an inflation and their earnings go to support families. Also, the ancient and honorable profession is suffering from the free-lance street competitors who call themselves Geishas—a stinging blow to bona fide Geisha Guild members.

The correspondents settled themselves in Romanesque ease while the piquant girls lit their cigarettes, poured *sake* from graceful porcelain bottles, and pressed food to their lips. The few moments of bliss we enjoyed were shattered by the interruption of wandering aviators from another room who thrust their crew-cut heads through the door, shouting, "Where are *our* Geishas?" and "How long do we have to wait?" to Momma-san. The "fly boys" returned to their own room only after she had assured them that girls for them were en route.

After dinner, the Geishas played the *samisen* and danced with exaggerated gestures and fan play, moving everything but their feet. Americans, attempting to follow the dance patterns, wove like giant bears among the tiny girls, endangering the rice-paper panel walls. As usual, I was put to work making sketches. The girls posed self-consciously and insisted I give the pictures to them.

By prearranged signal, the little Camilles of the kimono disappeared. A few minutes later the correspondents were guided by maids across the courtyard to a bathhouse. They tripped over flagstones, clumsy in the unaccustomed clogs they wore, spilling the whiskey they carried in glasses.

The Geishas were waiting in the warm, steamy interior, unclothed. I had not seen so many nudes since art-school days.

I sketched. Without clothing, they seemed even smaller with their short legs and tiny breasts. Their hair was gathered high to keep it from getting wet. They undressed the men and washed them with hot water from the sunken tile baths as they sat on ankle-high stools. The men were suddenly embarrassed. They smoked and drank their whiskey and tried not to look at the girls too subjectively. After washing, the men and girl couples steeped themselves in the deep tubs for a few minutes, Japanese style.

The Geishas dried the men with damp towels and draped them in crepe kimonos. Momma-san and the maids guided the men and their Geisha partners to tiny rooms. There they would become better acquainted.

In the morning, Momma-san and the maids appeared with tea and escorted their guests to the gate. They drove away to the fluttering of handkerchiefs and the waving of tiny hands.

In the plane to Korea that afternoon, the experience was relived many times.

6 • I Find a Student

Taegu's girls promenaded in springlike sunshine, their flowing blue and cerise silk gowns caught high under their breasts, giving their heavy forms an unsuspected grace. They drew wolf calls from hungry GI's. Spring was really on its way.

Women pounded shirts along the riverbank. ROK soldiers were singing as they drilled in crisp new uniforms. Market stalls were doing a fervent business in black-market cigarettes and Hershey bars.

Red Humphries, *Los Angeles Times* newsreelman, and I became co-owners of a jeep. For six bottles of Scotch, we bought the jeep from a motor-pool sergeant. Though it was bolted and welded together with parts from wrecked and scrapped jeeps, was difficult to start and had a cough, we were able at least to get a running start as we pointed north toward the fighting fronts.

Our spirits were high as we hit open country. The road was clear, nest-building birds sang from the trees, and we carried a cargo of Ballantine's three-ring brew and several cases of whiskey miniatures.

About midway, our dream of reaching the Han by nightfall was dissipated. Melting mountain snows had made Mississippis of every stream and rivulet in our path and we were slowed as we hit stretches of road that were under water. All bridges were swept away, forcing us to detour and seek fords. Our time problem was further aggravated when our jeep's cough became persistent and she dropped bolts.

It was night when we limped into an ordnance depot many miles short of our goal. A case of beer brought us a new radiator, crankshaft and tires. Beer-stimulated mechanics worked all night, giving the jeep a complete overhaul.

Next morning the jeep purred happily like a girl in a new mink coat as she twisted and turned through the last range of mountains separating us from the Han. The main bridge over the Han had given way to the flooding crest of the river a few minutes before we arrived. Two trucks had been caught on the bridge. They were partially submerged, only the tops of their cabs showing above water. Dozens of ammunition boxes were stranded on the shore. Army ducks were bringing shivering, soaked survivors to waiting ambulances and fires.

MP's detoured us to the Yoju ferry forty miles to the northwest. No luck there—ferry barges had been swept downriver by the angry flood. We jeeped fifteen miles to the ferry at Ch'onyang.

The torchlit scene at Ch'onyang ferry was hysterical. Trucks and jeeps, waiting to be ferried, were bumper to bumper on a precipitous road, slimy with mud, that led down to the shore. Ammunition trucks and ambulances with priorities wedged past them with difficulty.

A young engineer captain—who told us he had been without sleep for two nights—was working heroically to keep the stream of battle-bound traffic moving. As ferry barges propelled by ducks landed from the opposite shore, engineers quickly unloaded empty trucks and loaded ambulances. Vehicles waiting to cross were run aboard on inclined planks. The engineers, some of them working hip-deep in the icy water, shouted directions above the roar of the flood. Capacity loads sank the barges almost to the gunwales. Without the ducks lashed to either side, they would have foundered in the raging current.

Along about midnight, a huge British ammunition lorry was loaded. It left only space enough on the barge for a jeep. The captain waved us aboard. We gave him a box of Seagram miniatures which he distributed immediately to the men working in the freezing water.

I thought of Washington's crossing of the Delaware as we pushed through tossing blocks of ice toward the pin-point beams of flashlights on the opposite bank that guided us to a landing.

Headquarters of the 24th Division was within a few yards of the north-bank ferry landing. Before we turned in, we were invited to accompany a tank-supported patrol that was going out early the next morning.

The Chinese held a row of hills two thousand yards north of Pyong-yang, a town five miles down the river. The mission of the company-sized patrol was to take the hills.

Pink dawn was streaking the sky as we caught up with the patrol as it filed silently along a railroad embankment leading out of Pyong-yang. Avoiding the roads, the company deployed over rice paddies still covered with a thin crust of old snow, reconnoitering each farmhouse as we advanced over the utterly quiet landscape. The patrol dug in temporarily along a low ridge and waited for artillery and planes to commence their work of softening the enemy-held crests of hills directly across the narrow shallow valley.

Guns from tanks in the fields behind us opened the attack. Shells, panting as they sped overhead, wreathed the hilltops with bouquets of ghastly exploding roses. Corsairs, arriving precisely on schedule, joined the attack, dropping cylinders of napalm that torched the hills as they burst, and sent swirling clouds of black smoke to smudge the sky.

I had seen the first use of the jellied gasoline at St.-Malo in 1944. The Germans, holding its citadel, had somehow been forewarned of what was coming. Not caring for mass cremation, they

51

had surrendered a few minutes before the bombers arrived. The plane's fiery cargoes were diverted to the German-held isle of Cezembre off the coast. The smoking, burning island was proof of the success of this new weapon.

Now napalm was as much a part of warfare as shells and grenades. The burning oil splashes and spreads. It snakes down every path and crevice and over the lips of rifle pits, searching out and consuming every living thing, no matter how minute, animal or vegetable.

Through field glasses, we could see the contortions of burning men. To me it was like a writhing *Last Judgment* ballet, the music by Khachaturian.

Their work of burning done, the iron birds pointed fiery strings of tracer bullets at the fire they had set. Their ammunition finished, they plunged from sight beyond the mountains.

A platoon moved out across the valley below us and began toiling up the slopes of the smoking hills. I joined them.

The advance was slow and cautious. A lieutenant angrily shouted down men who ridge-walked or profiled themselves, if only for a moment. Paths were avoided because they might possibly be mined.

I kept close to a sergeant who resembled Victor McLaglen. He looked as though he had been through a dozen wars and could take good care of himself and everyone near him.

There was no live enemy on the first hilltop, but as a precaution, grenades were tossed into foxholes and tunnels. Bits of flesh and uniform sprayed from some of the pits. Progress on the next slope was slowed to a halt by small-arms fire from its crest. We dug in and waited for our artillery to silence it.

Shells, sounding like boxcars slamming together, broke over the enemy position. Shells, dropping short, forced us even deeper in our holes.

A heavy figure dove into the hollow I was sheltering in. From under the brim of my helmet, I squinted at a red-faced private who gasped, "This is it!" over and over again. Noting me, and evidently thinking that a uniformed man as gray and bearded as I must be a veteran of many battles, he nestled close to me. He shouted excitedly above the noise of bursting shells that he had arrived at the division only the night before:

"Christ, here I am—first day here and they've got me in the front lines!"

To put us both at ease, I questioned him. He told me he was Vince Del Buono, eighteen, from New York City. I replied that I was a New Yorker myself and asked him where he lived in the city. He gave me an address on First Avenue. I said I lived near First myself, only farther uptown. Did he go to school?

"I was planning to when they took me into the army. I want to be an artist. I was on the waiting list of the John Groth class at the Art Students League."

I told him he was an active member of the John Groth class as of this minute. His mouth opened in disbelief. I pulled out my sketch book and made a drawing for him. He was unconvinced. Perhaps the drawing didn't come up to his expectations of the teacher he had chosen. Finally, I showed him my dog tags. That clinched my identity for him.

He grinned and said, "Who'd have thought I would have to come all the way to Korea to get into your class. Guess you don't have a waiting list here!"

I noticed that he no longer nestled as close as when he had thought I was a bona fide soldier. An art teacher is hardly a guy to fight alongside!

The artillery show over, Vince rejoined his squad. I heard from him recently. He had been hit in the ankle by a sniper's bullet five minutes after the action and is a civilian again. He is studying art but with another teacher in another school. The sketch I made for him on a Central Korean hill must have changed his mind.

We found many dead on the hilltop. Torn and bloody Chinese were splashed everywhere among the scrub pine. There were a few souvenirs—a Chinese officer's notebook (which none of the boys could read), a pair of tennis shoes that were grabbed by a footsore private, a tommy gun and several rifles. I picked up a carbine. I had been weaponless thus far in the war. Most correspondents carried weapons. Their noncombatant status is not respected by guerrillas. The feel of a carbine in the crook of my arm was psychologically reassuring.

The platoon trekked downhill in good spirits. The mission had been successfully accomplished without a casualty. Thirsty men dipped their emptied canteens into the first spring we crossed. The lieutenant warned them that the water might be contaminated. Halazone tablets were dropped into the canteens. A corporal who had already drunk a canteenful of the stream's water quickly swallowed a half dozen of the tablets.

7 · Mash 8063

Action flamed suddenly along the entire front as UN troops began a new advance against a fanatical enemy holding range after range of mountains. Every hill gained was bought by casualties. The roads leading from the front were filled with ambulances.

I found Mobile Army Surgical Hospital ("MASH") 8063 in a mountain-rimmed valley near Chong-won-ni, a quarter-mile quadrangle of khaki circus and pyramid tents pitched over sand-filled paddies.

Within the quadrangle was a beehive of activity, ambulances darting in and being unloaded by teams of corpsmen, engineers stringing communications wire, Korean helpers carrying tubs of water and piling drums of gasoline. Helicopters rose and settled on a tiny strip and, a half mile away, giant evac planes carrying wounded men to base hospitals in the rear took off moments apart.

Inside the circus-like tents, drama was being enacted hour by hour, night and day. It was late in the day and the "return traffic" of war was unusually heavy. Litter bearers waited outside the overflowing receiving tent until space was created for their burden of wounded. Inside no cot was empty. Ambulatory wounded stood in the long aisles, supporting each other or huddled on the sand near the stove. As always, pain here was democratic. A dying North Korean POW was flanked by wounded Americans, all three of them receiving blood from bottles suspended above their cots. There was a grouping of Australians, Greeks, Canadians, and Chinese POW's. A pregnant Korean peasant woman, with a sick coughing baby on her back, humbly waited until one of the frantically busy nurses could find a moment to give her bronchial baby attention.

No one is turned away from MASH. Korean villagers, from miles around, brought in their sick and injured who received the same treatment as UN soldiers, though sometimes they had to wait. Soldiers are treated first.

All patients—civilians as well as soldiers—were stripped, cleaned and deloused with DDT immediately after entering the tent. Piles of wet and muddy clothes were burnt in a field near the camp. (The clothes were searched carefully for weapons. Some soldiers, particularly the Greeks, carry grenades in their pockets. Weapons taken from the soldiers are returned to quartermaster supply. My armament was augmented by a Colt .45 from the weapon pile.)

Most wounded bore their pain stolidly and silently. Some were even able to joke through their pain. A Negro private was jubilant despite his bandaged left hand. When two sergeants sprinkled DDT over his long brown body and hair—there was so much powder on his hair that he looked as if he were wearing an 18th century wig—he exclaimed over and over again, "I got the noncoms waiting on me now."

Patients continued to arrive all through the night. As fast as men were prepared for surgery and carried to the operating tent, ambulances arrived as if on schedule. I sketched an Australian, his leg shattered above the knee, who refused to let litter bearers carry him to the operating room unless he could take his cherished bush hat with him. He entered the surgical tent with the hat clutched on his breast.

I also sketched a Communist-hating Greek who tried to hurl himself from his litter to attack a wounded POW, though his arms and chest were heavily bandaged and his right leg was in a splint. It took the combined strength of two corpsmen and a nurse to hold him. Bloody ribbons of bandage, loosened by his struggle, flapped about him as the hysterical Greek screamed death threats and curses at the wounded prisoner.

Toward midnight, a Korean boy entered the tent, carrying a little girl. Her left upper arm was festering from an ugly wound. Space was made for her immediately on a cot. Doll-like ten-year-old Si Ki had been wounded by a strafing UN plane a week before. This was the first time her wound had been tended. He brother, Kim Tai Sik, refused to leave her. The serious-faced thirteen-year-old boy never moved from her side while she was in the hospital. He kept a constant vigil, standing very erect. After Si Ki's operation, he slept in a blanket on the ground beside her bed until she was evacuated to a Korean hospital.

A few minutes after the children arrived, a picturesque old peasant limped into the tent, using his wife as a crutch. He had a week-old, untended shrapnel wound in his leg. He wore a pointed beard and a Cossack-type black caracul hat cocked rakishly over one eye. All eyes in the tent were on him. He was pleased with the attention. He was as interested in the men about him as they were in him. Despite corpsmen's and nurses' efforts to keep him down, he insisted upon sitting bolt upright in his bed. He didn't want to miss any of the intense activity. GI's slipped him a roll of colored Life Savers and a cigarette. He smoked the cigarette cockily and crunched the candy with noisy pleasure.

His drab, dutiful wife squatted on the ground, watching only him. He gave her one of the Life Savers with a kingly gesture. A look of real hurt came over his face when a nurse took the cigarette and candy away from him.

There was a space of an hour when no ambulances arrived and the tent's feverish activity died down, giving the tired nurses time to relax and drink a cup of needed coffee. Lieutenant Pettrina Mead of Frankfort, Mich., walked over with a cup of coffee to watch me complete my sketch of the picturesque peasant. The lulling strains of Brahms' *Lullaby* quieted the wounded. The sergeant in charge of the registration desk asked if I had a favorite. The portable record player belonged to him. The music helped corpsmen, nurses and patients during the long night.

I selected *The Dance of the Little Swans* from Tchaikovsky's *Swan Lake*. It was conducted by my friend, Leopold Stokowski.

Pretty Lieutenant Ruth Nichols of Brooklyn, N. Y., divided her time between two sleepless wounded. She talked tenderly to a badly burned American tankman whose head and hands were completely covered with bandage. His eyes followed her lips through thin slits in the head bandage. She helped me entertain Sergeant Charles Tripp of Greenville, Tenn., who was most uncomfortable.

58

The cast that wrapped him from waist to neck forced him to sit erect. He asked me to make a sketch of Lieutenant Nichols on his cast. I did my best. She autographed it for the sergeant.

None of the soldiers had seen an American girl for many months. It helped them forget their pain, somewhat, to talk to them. Though the nurses had been working at a killing pace, they managed to look attractive, despite heavy Army clothing and combat boots. Their lipstick was on straight, their hair neat.

Just before dawn, the tempo of the tent quickened. The nurses dropped their coffee cups and went into action again as an ambulance discharged a load of mangled First Cavalry men. A grenade, dropping into a campfire from a careless GI's breast pocket, had exploded, killing three men and wounding eleven.

(The same kind of accident occurred the next day when another grenade exploded in a campfire. A goodly proportion of casualties at war result from accidents, carelessly handled weapons, overturning jeeps and drownings.)

I felt guilty leaving the tired corpsmen and nurses when I reeled to bed at five A.M. My last waking thought was of the cheerful sergeant who owned the record player. He had told me this was his second night without sleep.

I spent the next morning in the surgical tent. A crew of tall surgeons—as big as Kansas U basketball players—headed by Major Keith Walker of Portland, Ore., operated on an endless stream of patients who were carried into the dirt-floored tent without letup.

The tent in which they worked was hardly the operating theatre of a modern American hospital. Instead of sterile white, the doctors wore khaki fatigues and black rubber aprons. The only white was that of face masks (a nurse had tied one over my mouth) and the sheets that covered tables and draped the tent's walls. They worked under bare light bulbs as, with a minimum of instruments, they performed intricate operations. I saw them amputate the shell-torn feet of a soldier, within twenty minutes after he had been prepared for surgery. In this instance, Dr. Walker told me, speed was of the utmost importance. The operation had to be completed before severe shock set in. I sketched while shell fragments were removed from vicious chest and belly wounds. My layman's stomach weakened at times. The sight of a Negro soldier's horribly shredded testicles—from a shell fragment—was almost too much for me.

It was not so difficult to sketch attractive Captain Kathryn Doody of Salisbury, Md., giving pentothal sodium or newly arrived Lieutenant Arthur Driscoll of Boston, Mass., applying a cast to the broken leg of a South Korean.

I sketched several patients with comparatively slight wounds. As the doctors probed and trimmed their wounds, they joked and commented on my sketches. A fresh crew of surgeons and nurses entered the tent. The doctors and nurses who had been working steadily for the last three hours, staggered outside, slumped wearily on boxes and lit cigarettes. It had been a long morning for them.

Lunch was being served in the post-op wards when I visited them. In the soldier ward, a sweatered nurse of very generous proportions was helping morale as she joked and served chicken, mashed potatoes and cherry pie. Even some of the more painfully wounded broke into laughter during the tent-wide ribbing of her. Lieutenant Eileen Maloney of Mobile, Ala., who responded to "Alabama" and "Irish," kidded them back, as she cracked, "My boy friend's a tankman" and "I got a tank deal working."

Most of the wounded men had been through the worst of their ordeal and were awaiting evacuation to hospitals in Japan. They looked forward to recovery and, possibly, a leave in Tokyo before their return home.

In the meantime, American boys were becoming acquainted with British and Greek boys. They were interested in the sketches I was doing and asked me to add drawings to the letters many

of them were writing. They insisted I draw "Alabama." She lost her poise as she posed blushingly. I slimmed down her lines in my sketch. That delighted her. She showed the picture to every patient in the big tent.

The other post-op tent held POW's and Korean civilians. Some were enjoying the strange-to-them American food while others ate only the bread and asked for rice instead. In the first cot, a little naked girl with a bandage wound about her head sat on a blanket surrounded by American and Korean corpsmen: nine-year-old Kang Chong-he was eating oranges as fast as corpsman Pfc. Anslen Stamnitz of Austin, Tex., peeled them. She wore his wrist watch on her thin upper arm.

Near the rear of the tent, petite Lieutenant Zita Irieno of Chicago, Ill., was trying without success to ease a sick Korean peasant woman who rocked back and forth in her cot as she sobbed.

Colonel James M. Brown, of Omaha, Neb., 8063's commanding officer, entered the tent to ask me if I would like to go on a helicopter mission to pick up a casualty north of Yoju. I was eager to go.

Captain Arne Eliasson of Bedford, N. Y., took off immediately. The plexiglass bubble we sat in afforded perfect observation. I had the sensation of being in a suspended goldfish bowl. We were wafted gently over checkerboard rice fields and wandering ranges of hills.

The "flying windmills" are able to land in any clearing large enough to allow their rotary blades to revolve. They can land on ice or snow, enabling the evacuation of wounded men sometimes practically in the front lines. The precious time saved between pickup and operating table has preserved many UN soldiers' lives. An ambulance trip taking hours can be accomplished in minutes by helicopter.

A bright orange panel, shining from a snow-covered rice paddy, guided us to the casualty. A large group of soldiers waited near the panel. As the 'copter gently grounded, they approached slowly, carrying a stretcher. A corpsman, keeping pace with the litter, administered blood to the unconscious officer. The blanket folded under his head was crimson with blood. Many of the men attending him were crying. They carefully placed him in one of the helicopter's litter baskets.

60

I had stepped from the 'copter when we landed. The corpsman climbed into my vacated seat and continued to administer blood. In a few moments, the little plane was lost from sight as it flew swiftly on its lifesaving mission.

I walked with the grieving enlisted men and officers to their tents. They were combat engineers. The seriously wounded officer was a popular captain who had been with the battalion from the day they landed in Korea.

A half hour before the helicopter's arrival, a rifle bullet, accidentally discharged from a GI's gun, had passed through a tent wall and struck the captain in his right temple—another war accident! The camp was desolated by the unfortunate tragedy. The private whose carelessness had caused this was inconsolable. There was nothing now that they could do but pray that surgery might save their captain's life.

I accompanied a party of the men back to MASH 8063. When we arrived, Dr. Walker told us that the captain had died on the operating table.

It took me two days to gain entry to the nurses' tent. Chief Nurse Major Helen Lyons of Columbus, O., gave me permission, but with the proviso that I give ten minutes' notice before each entry—this to give the nurses time to take their female unmentionables from the clothesline and put them on.

I sent my warning message but it evidently had not been delivered when I entered the tent. My visit surprised them. Several sat up in bed and rubbed sleep from their eyes. A few others ducked behind the protection of clotheslines draped with long johns, bras, panties and stockings. One girl hung over the edge of a cot, washing her hair in a helmet. I identified her as Captain Thelma Kiltz of Long Beach, Cal., when she raised her dripping head.

Some of the girls slept on despite the excitement my entry caused. Some of the fully-dressed girls were packing bedrolls. They were leaving with an advance echelon setting up a new MASH at Yoju. The front was moving and MASH was following. Others sat on the edges of their cots,

drinking Coca Colas and reading pocket magazines. They all wore shapeless baggy wool pajamas, tucked into thick wool socks. One girl was patting her flanks as she warmed herself against the gasoline stove. The novelty of a man in the tent—they told me I was the first since they had come to Korea—soon wore off. They relaxed and talked freely to me.

The tent was the same as soldier tents, the same cots, stoves and celluloid windows. The girls kept their belongings and cosmetics in wooden boxes beside their cots. There was an end table, made of ammunition boxes and boards and covered neatly with Kleenexes, that bore most of the amenities of nurse life in Korea—a cocktail shaker, cameras, cartons of cigarettes, perfumes, insecticides, and a cake from home. Like soldiers, the nurses had pin-ups. Over the end table they had hung a double-page spread from *Esquire* displaying the Mr. America finalists flexing their muscular charms on a Florida beach.

They told me that the helmet hanging at every cot end was "a girl's best friend." Only two wash basins had been furnished to the sixteen girls in the tent so the helmet became a portable bath and a laundry tub.

The girls' clothes are regulation GI olive drab. In the winter they wear wool underwear. They dream of silk undies and skirts. They wear colored parachute scarves to lighten the monotonous drabness of combat clothes and their touches of "Shalimar" and "Chanel #5" sweeten the air of a countryside famous for its unpleasant odor. They live like soldiers, the same clothes, the same food. They stand in chow lines. Kiltz told me that at times the food froze to their mess kits before they could reach their tent to eat it.

"Many's the time we ate sitting on paddy banks or on ambulance fenders," she said.

She told me that when the weather is really Arctic, they crawl, fully clothed, into their sleeping bags.

62

When the nurses were rushed to Korea, they were faced with conditions no other group of American women had ever experienced. There were no clean hospital buildings to receive the wounded, no beds with white sheets, nothing. Complete hospital units had to be organized and begin work immediately in what is one of the world's most unsanitary countries. They moved forward and backward with the rising and falling fortunes of the UN armies. In a matter of hours, they had to set up shop and begin their merciful work: wounded men cannot wait. Sometimes they had to lie in ditches when guerrillas sniped at their ambulance convoys. Once the 8063 nurses had to pitch their tent over a cotton field. They had to pick the cotton before they could pitch the tents.

Korean civilians coming to the hospital add to their problems. Sometimes entire families accompany the sick member. Kiltz told me about a nurse who had been working continuously for sixty hours and was so slap-happy with fatigue that she bandaged two healthy relatives as well as their injured kinsman.

Despite all the hardship under which they lived and worked, their morale was high. It has to be when sixteen girls live together in a single tent under primitive conditions. They make a brave attempt to have some of the pleasures of normal girl existence. They have parties, they make events of birthdays within the group, they date, they become engaged and marry (at least some of them), they adopt pets. The 8063 girls own a pony-size dog who avoids them, remembering a bath they gave him. They make clothes for the Korean orphan adopted by the camp. They have a radio and they sing the same songs the soldiers do, the songs inspired by Korea which will never be heard on radio programs back home, let me add. They do a lot of healthy kidding about their trials and tribulations. "DDT" ("Drop dead twice") in their language is answered with "DDDS" ("Don't drop dead—suffer").

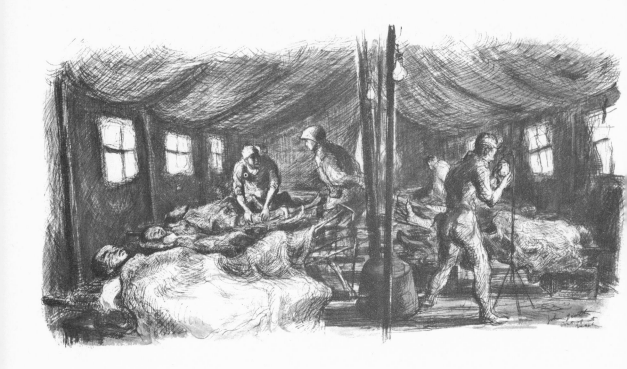

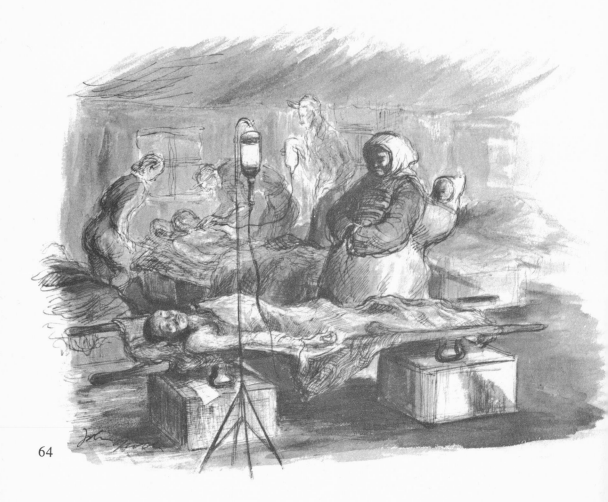

Nurses sightseeing
in Suwon
Korea

Enlisted men and Koreans were striking tents when I staggered out of bed the next morning at six-thirty. MASH was moving to Yoju to join its advanced echelon. A mass exodus was on. Cots, operating tables, X-ray machines were loaded onto trucks and trailers. The linesmen were taking down the precious wire. Shouting Korean boys rolled gas drums to the road's edge. Soldiers pulling at ropes brought the tents to the sand. They were quickly folded and put on the trucks. A gallery of villagers watched. Flyers from the air strip were saying goodbye to the nurses. One girl was kissed long and affectionately.

Soon the convoy of trucks and ambulances were on their way north to Yoju.

8 · Heroes, Exarhos and Opie

Greek soldiers took time out to color Easter eggs the day after they won a spectacular victory. The Canadians were bloodied in their first Korean action but effectively revenged themselves the next day. Madly fighting Australians discarded their pile caps and wore their bush hats into a murderous battle on a craggy mountain top.

Red Humphries and I recrossed the Han at Yoju, on our way to visit the "foreign" brigades. We stopped at the far end of a newly installed pontoon bridge to watch ragged Chinese prisoners drag a truck from a ditch. A captain and a girl soldier were among them. Both received the full attention of curious American GI's. A captured Chinese officer was a rarity: a Chinese WAC even rarer. All of the prisoners were bedraggled and battle-shocked. Despite her dirty, shapeless, padded uniform, the girl was proud and pretty. Her aloofness was softened by the cigarettes and ration cans generous GI's pressed into her chapped hands. She smiled and everyone laughed, including the Chinese prisoners.

We found the Greeks at Chip-yong-ni, twenty miles to the north. They were in bivouac after their headline-making charge of the day before.

An English-speaking Greek officer guided us to a nearby village to meet the hero of the attack, Corporal Panageotıs Exarhos of Athens. The thatched-roof farm buildings constituted a Greek island in a muddy sea of Korean paddies.

Our entry into a courtyard interrupted the daily shave of Private Panageotis Panageotopoulos of Tripoli. He was holding his helmet as a shaving basin while former Athens barber, Corporal Basil Stathopoulos, scraped away the beard and dirt of the last few days. The Greek barbershop scene was complete. Soldiers, waiting their turn for haircuts and shaves, sat under the Greek flag, reading the Attic equivalents of the *Police Gazette* and *Esquire* as chickens pecked at their shoes. Corporal Stathopoulos's "shop" was fully equipped from the open razor that flashed with the gestures that accompanied his running barbershop conversation to a row of bottles containing olive oil, shampoo and brilliantine.

In their GI uniforms, the Greeks might have been mistaken for American soldiers. Only their swarthy mustached faces and excited gestures distinguished them from their Yankee comrades. I was introduced to several of the ten-syllable-name soldiers while we waited for Corporal Exarhos to make his appearance. The friendly soldiers offered us cigarettes and Greek candy and brought up boxes for us to sit on. They talked of yesterday's attack, underplaying their own roles and speaking enthusiastically of Exarhos's exploits. Without doubt, the corporal had attained an Olympian eminence among his comrades.

Exarhos appeared with a retinue of admiring fellow soldiers. He saluted grandly and stood at rigid attention when he saw us. We asked him to tell us about his part in the attack.

The tall, handsome, twenty-six-year-old Athenian grew animated as he described the "attack." He supplemented his word picture with action, brandishing an M-3 submachine gun and "throwing" grenades he pulled from his pockets.

He had led the uphill assault under heavy enemy fire, cleaning out rifle pits and hurling grenades to all points of the compass. He had forced the pace of the attack so rapidly that, within minutes, the Greeks had been on the summit of the hill and the Chinese were fleeing down the reverse slope. (A sergeant interrupted to describe the scene they had found at the top—Corporal Exarhos, astride a rifle pit, waving a grenade at a terrified Chinese infantryman who waved a white cloth of surrender as he begged for his life. Only a lieutenant's command had stopped him from throwing the grenade.) Exarhos modestly waved aside the heavy share of credit given him for the success of the attack. He remarked, "We cheered and shouted so loud as we came up the hill that the Communists must have thought the whole Greek army was coming at them."

The hysterics of Communist-hating Greek attacks were well known along the front. They pray, scream, curse and shout insults in fanatically mad dashes through the heaviest fire. The Greeks, more than any other UN soldiers, hated the Communist enemy. All of the Greek Expeditionary Force were volunteers. Most of them had fought in civil war at home; they knew Communism firsthand and detested it. I remembered the wounded Greek soldier at MASH 8063 who had tried to attack a North Korean POW from his stretcher, despite his bandaged arms and splinted leg.

As the interview ended, we were joined by one of the most extraordinary figures I had seen anywhere in Korea, five-foot-high Lieutenant Valetellis Neophitos of Athens, Chaplain of the Greek Expeditionary Force. He was probably the most unmilitary figure with the UN Army. The priest's rich curling brown beard reached to the waist of his British battle dress. His long hair escaped in waves from under his overseas cap. He carried an unfurled black umbrella everywhere, no matter what the weather. I had met him for the first time on a flight from Tokyo to Taegu. He had been airsick every minute of the trip. Though flying made him violently ill, he flew to every part of Korea and Japan, wherever there were wounded Greek soldiers to comfort.

Neophitos invited us into the CP for refreshments. Inside we found fierce-looking Greeks tinting Easter eggs for the Orthodox holiday. Heavy chapped fingers handled the eggs tenderly as they dyed them pink and blue, red and yellow. Some of the soldiers copied motifs from the ikons that shared the walls with battle-terrain maps. Others painted tiny crosses and the blue and white Greek flag on their eggs. They removed their pile caps and crossed themselves as the little priest blessed their holy labors. We sat around a Greek brazier, sipping anisette and eating olives and cloyingly sweet Greek candies.

When we left, Father Neophitos blessed us and presented us with colored eggs, giving Humphries a red one that matched his hair.

From Chip-yong-ni to the Canadians at Kosong-ni was but a fifteen-mile jaunt due east, according to our maps. We had no reason to believe that the road passed through enemy-held territory.

70

The MP directing traffic at Chip-yong-ni's main crossroad waved us on to it.

The bleak valleys we drove through were quiet. Not even the chirping of a bird broke the silence. We wondered at the absence of American military traffic. A "situation map" we had seen the night before had shown First Cavalry units holding it, but the only inhabitants we saw, in an hour of jeeping, were a clump of dead Chinese soldiers. Their contorted bodies had been twisted by napalm fire into sculpture. Their fire-blackened skulls grinned at us as we passed. We wondered why they hadn't been buried.

After another mile of creepy quiet, we came upon more dead Chinese bodies. We slowed down as we nearly ran over one lying in the road. Simultaneously, we looked at each other and said, "Let's go back!"

Red turned the jeep quickly and kept his foot on the accelerator as we careened back the way we had come.

Back at the Chip-yong-ni crossroad, the MP who had waved us on to the road signaled us to a stop, and yelled, "Holy smoke, where are you guys coming from? That's no man's land!"

He denied having directed us, he denied ever having seen us before. He went on to tell us that our jeep was the first vehicle to come out of the road since a patrol, reporting enemy guerrillas, had come out early in the morning. He put us on a "safe" road leading south.

Fifty miles of backtracking and detours were ahead of us before we reached the Canadians. I added another MP traffic "wrongo" to the long list I had compiled in two wars.

After lunch back at Yoju, we followed a main supply route leading north. All along the route we were delayed by floods. Never-ending files of Korean peasants carried baskets on their heads filled with the gravel and stones engineers were using to repair the road.

At one point we passed a big mound of bloodied sleeping bags. A soldier near them told us they were the bags that had belonged to a Negro combat engineer outfit that had been wiped out by enemy night attack. The exhausted engineers had crawled into their sleeping bags after a day of

New Zealand Artillery
near Rosonga-mi

fighting, leaving only a light guard. Just before dawn the enemy had returned, surprising them in their sleep. The Negro soldiers were murdered before they were able to unzip their bags.

We had only time enough for a short visit with Troop B of the Royal New Zealand Artillery. Their guns were set up in paddies on the edge of a typical Korean village. Peasant life was proceeding as usual about them. Expressionless Korean men and women carried water jars and led oxen in seeming disregard of the pounding field pieces.

I had seen a similar vignette in the Siegfried Line where German peasants had harvested their potatoes in fields among booming American 105's.

To the village's children, the New Zealanders and their artillery were an exciting diversion. Boys and girls crowded about the cannon, imitating the gunners' actions and holding their ears at each explosion. They were underfoot and in the way of the artillerymen. When shouted away, they ran, but always surged back. Heavy red-mustached Sergeant Jock MacGregor of Wellington and his crew joined us in a drink. (We still had a box of the Seagram's miniatures.)

Both he and Corporal Les Hughes of Auckland voiced the artilleryman's frustration of hardly ever seeing the shells they fired registering on their targets.

"We might as well be blind men," said Hughes.

The entire crew accommodated us in our picturemaking, my sketches and Red's newsreel shots. Each man described his work and they fired several "uncalled-for" rounds at the enemy.

The children crowded about us as we worked. They were not frightened off by MacGregor's oaths. They knew his bluff good nature too well. Our pictures finished, we toasted them with more miniatures and were on our way.

It was late afternoon when we reached the Princess Pat's farmhouse CP. It was ringed with press jeeps. A British mortar battery banged shells in a field next to it. Bearded British and Canadian correspondents warmed themselves at a fire outside the house. They drank tea and discussed the bloody baptism the Canadians had received that morning in their first action.

Red-bearded Canadian reporter Bill Boss told us that the Canadians had carried the first slope of their mountain objective easily and without casualties. The success of the first phase of their operation excited them and they charged prematurely from the cover of trees at the edge of the snow line only to run into an ambush. Machine-gun fire killed and wounded most of the men in the first squads. The company retreated, carrying their wounded but leaving their dead.

The Australians, on the right of the Pats, had taken their objective. The boastful Anzacs had taunted the Canadians, making unfavorable comparisons between the success of the two actions. This had rankled the Pats and they were now resolved to pass out bloody noses to the Chinese on their second attack tomorrow morning.

I climbed a slippery path to reach a machine-gun nest on a hill overlooking the CP. I found Private Joe McGillivary crouched behind a Vickers. The Cree Indian from Cumberland House, Saskatchewan, was searching with eagle eyes the enemy slopes opposite. Whenever he saw or thought he saw movement, he fired. He was already knee-deep in empty clips. I facetiously asked him if he planned to scalp the enemy he was shooting. He gave me a quick look and answered with a grin, "Chinamen shave their heads—what good are scalps without hair?"

I was probably the tenth color-story-hungry correspondent that day to bother him with silly questions of scalps and war whoops. He bent seriously to his work and I left him.

I followed a bearded Bunyanesque Canadian giant up a wooded road. He carried a heavy mine detector as casually as if it were a cane. He led me uphill where I found Dog Company preparing to send a patrol into a valley below to recover the body of a slain comrade. Through field glasses, I could see the dead Canadian lying spread-eagled over a burial mound in a small Korean cemetery. While the patrol readied itself for the mission, I made the acquaintance of some of the "GI's from over the border" as American soldiers call them.

Private William Love of Porcupine Plain, Saskatchewan, had the distinction of being the first Canadian to kill a Chinese soldier. He, like most of the Canadians, was a big, rangy outdoor type who looked as if he might have stepped from the covers of *Field and Stream*. Most of the Pats had fished and hunted in the north woods all of their lives. They were conditioned to cold weather and rigorous activity. Love, who had hunted big game, said killing Chinese was no different from shooting a moose.

Private Robert C. Campbell of Calgary, Alberta, liked fishing.

"I'm sending home for my rod and flies. I know there are speckled trout in these mountain streams," he told me.

Private Willis Baker of Corner Brook, Newfoundland, who was a cod fisherman, sneered at what he considered a panty-waist sport. I mistook Private William Lee of Lethbridge, Alberta, for

Pvt. William Love
of Porcupine Plain, Saskatchewan

an Eskimo. His Mongolian face was framed in a fur-trimmed parka. He answered, "No, I'm Chinese, but I guess I'm the nearest thing to an Eskimo in Dog Company."

Tall, handsome Private Gordon Austin of London, Ontario, who held a canteen cup of coffee as if he were posing for the Man of Distinction ads, was here, as he said, "for adventure." The same statement made in an American squad would have brought jeers. Here, it brought no comment.

Austin had seen six years of war in India and Burma. He had enlisted in the Pats when the Canadian government called for Korea volunteers. He had been in Ottawa on holiday at the time.

The patrol was soon lost to sight in the forest. It reappeared a half hour later in the open country near the graveyard. At about the same moment, the sharp eyes of a Cree private detected enemy observers looking down at the patrol from a commanding height. I looked through his glasses and saw two white figures leaning out of a pine-branch-camouflaged slit trench. I could see their binoculars as they followed the Canadian patrol's movements. A lieutenant called for artillery fire over the walkie-talkie. Soon the slit trench was bracketed with mortar fire. When it stopped, we could see no more telltale movement.

The patrol below had dodged behind burial mounds when the firing began. Now they quickly lifted the body and commenced their return trip. When they arrived at Dog Company CP, I saw that their faces were crisscrossed with scratches from low-hanging branches.

Just after dawn, formations of planes poured napalm on the Canadians' mountain objective. Their wing cannon stabbed rockets into the fire. Shells from New Zealand and British guns added more fire. During the bombardment, Dog Company commenced its climb up paths slimy from rain. The heavily laden men were able to ascend at times only by pulling themselves up by grasping bushes and branches.

I followed the squad I had met the day before. Yesterday's chilling experience made for greater caution today. Progress was slow and there were frequent halts as patrols probed. No advances were made until the area immediately ahead was secure.

The point squads above were meeting resistance. There was the furious sound of small arms fire and the sudden grunt of grenades. As the squad left the protection of the trees and crossed into the snow line, we passed the dead Canadians of yesterday's ambush. They had been stripped of parkas, shoes and gloves. Soldiers murmured names of their dead comrades as they identified them.

A bit further up, near a rock face, a soldier hugged his wounded chest. Blood welled over his sleeves. A corpsman knelt beside him. We heard shouting above. A cerise panel gleamed hotly on the snow of the crest and Canadians were profiled against the sky.

When we reached the top, we could see that the artillery and napalm had done its work. Scorched pieces of dead Chinese hung on bushes and were scattered everywhere.

"Never saw so much fresh meat," a sergeant exclaimed, "not outside a slaughter house."

The Pats had delivered a really bloody nose.

The victorious Pats set about cleaning up the mess. They were going to occupy the foxholes. The enemy would certainly counterattack. The bits of Chinese were shoveled from pits and pushed over cliff edges. There was surprisingly little griping over the ugly job.

A corporal opined, "At least it saves us some digging. My back is grateful."

While we mounted the peak, the Australians were engaged in a heavy attack to our right. From our hilltop we had balcony seats and a perfect view of the last act. They crawled up the craggy mountain as fast as ants, scaling sheer rock faces sometimes with bare handholds. They fired from behind rocks with only their rifles and heads showing, as they shot at the winking lights of fire from Chinese rifle pits. As they neared the top, the big-hatted Australians reared up, threw their grenades, and dropped quickly behind boulders. Sometimes they were silhouetted against snowbanks. When the wind was blowing in our direction, we could hear their shouts.

For a few moments they were lost in the clouds of smoke that wreathed the summit. When we saw them again, they were on the topmost ridge.

As I left the Canadians, an icy rain began to fall and the foxholes and rifle pits began to fill. I didn't envy them the night ahead on the mountain. I reached the snow line as the dead at its edge were placed tenderly on ponchos and litters and carried down as gently as though they were still alive.

The Australians were jubilant when I reached their CP. This was their second victory in two days. Red and I contributed Ballantines and Four Roses to the celebration. The big, rawboned Anzacs were still appealing even when they were boasting about their prowess in battle, in bars and in bed. It was easy for me to see why they are called the "Texans of the British Commonwealth." They wore the Australian version of the ten-gallon hat with great pride and the hats were as individually shaped and crumpled as their wearers could make them. They loved the flexible felts. I offered one owner a crisp $20 bill for his dirty, hole-punctured campaign hat but he refused it with disdain. I don't think the Australian boy I saw carried into the operating room, his hat clutched to his breast, would have sold his either.

I asked one of the big red-faced men what was so valuable to him about the hat he was wearing.

"Keeps the sun out of my eyes and the rain off my neck. It's the best friend I got in Korea," he replied.

The free-wheeling Aussies enjoy their rough-neck reputation and try to live up to it at all times. When the "tough" soldiers were ordered to change socks several times daily during the winter to avoid frostbitten feet, they disregarded the order as "sissy." As a result, they suffered more frostbite cases than any of the other more strictly disciplined UN groups.

A massive, walrus-mustached corporal, bristling with guns, loomed into the CP. The soldiers hailed him and slapped him on the back as if he were a boxing champ entering his dressing room. He was Lem Opie of Medindie, South Australia, the star of today's epic assault. At first he was as closemouthed as Joe Louis but the whiskey and beer soon loosened the lips under the shaggy blond mustache.

While I sketched Opie, he described his afternoon's work.

"I led my section up the mountainside. When we got up to the first line of pits, the Chinos began throwin' grenades. One of 'em bobbed out of a pit near me with his arm raised ready to throw. I fired my Owen as the grenade came at me." (It had been slung over his right shoulder and he was firing it from his hip. He had been carrying a Lee Enfield in the other hand.) "I twisted sideways so it didn't get me. Another Chino about 50 yards away hopped up with a stick grenade. I gave him two bursts with the Owen but missed him. Shot him with the rifle. The other one was still movin' so I emptied my Owen on him. I took the Chino's Thompson submachine gun and kept firin' until it jammed. I threw the Thompson away. There was blood and stuff on it. The rest of the platoon came up even with me. We went to the second ridge about 50 yards along a saddle, cleanin' out the pits as we went. I followed Charlie Thorburn and Ozzie Hughes who was carrying a Bren gun. I saw a Chino put a rifle muzzle out of one of the holes and sang out, 'Get down, Charlie!' But he got Charlie in the right shoulder and knocked Ozzie down. I pulled back about 30 feet behind some rocks and exchanged grenades with him. Got 'im. Then I took his M-1 and fired the remaining round along the other side of the saddle. The M-1 was empty. I tossed it away and picked up a carbine. We got to the top. Then, when they began firin' at us from another peak, we moved back down a bit on our side. We stayed there until another company relieved us. As we were carrying Ozzie down, he died. This is his Bren gun. What an afternoon!"

I agreed that it *had* been quite an afternoon. I checked the arsenal he had used in an hour's fighting. As well as grenades, he had used an Owen, a Lee Enfield, a Thompson submachine gun, an M-1, a carbine and a Bren gun.

As we walked out the door, Red, visibly impressed, muttered to me, "By God, I hope the Aussies are on our side in *every* war!"

9 · Bubble Gum-san in Arcadia

During my twenty years as an artist, I've had many different kinds of studios. I did my first drawings on the kitchen table at home on wrapping paper from the butcher shop downstairs. After art school, I had a "depression" studio in Chicago's Bohemia, in a building filled with struggling painters, poets, ballerinas and musicians. I've worked in a Greenwich Village loft and in a stucco mansion on the Normandy beachhead. During World War II, I had a succession of studios across the ETO—a stable at St. Sauveur, a castle at Laval, a glamorous two-story-high affair with a balcony in the heart of Paris's Montparnasse (given me by French artists who had "liberated" it from a collaborator) and a farmhouse in the Siegfried Line with Ernest Hemingway as a roommate.

But perhaps the most unusual studio I've had to date was my atelier on a Japanese farm surrounded by a sea of rice with a one-legged chicken as a mascot and the whole countryside as a gallery.

I found the studio just outside the village of Teigo near Kasukabe in the Saitama Prefecture after my Japanese artist friends had searched all of Tokyo, without success, to find me one.

My Korea sketchbooks were overflowing. I needed a place to work, desperately, so that I could translate my notes into drawings and paintings. It was impossible for me to work in the noisy, overcrowded Correspondents' Club. Like any other artist, I needed space and quiet.

My friend, Nioshi Keneko, had a sudden inspiration. He knew a well-to-do farmer in the Teigo neighborhood who had liked an American writer so much he had built him a summerhouse in which he had worked one year immediately after the war. Keneko thought he might invite me to stay there if he liked me enough. He suggested that we visit Tonahichi Iwamoto and see. Keneko felt a bottle of Scotch would help greatly.

We packed ourselves and the whiskey into a jeep and set off. As we cleared the city's suburbs, the sun burst brilliantly over the billiard-table flat landscape of the Tokyo plain.

Gayly colored strips of freshly dyed silk fluttered from bamboo poles. Plump babies in parti-colored kimonos played like butterflies in the clover. Bigger boys and girls flew kites and rolled hoops along the road's edge. The snow on distant Fujiyama's cone glittered against a deep blue sky. The fragile little wooden houses that bordered the road were open to the sun. I caught fleeting tableaux of grandfathers and grandmothers smoking long silver pipes and mothers kneeling before babies, feeding them with chopsticks.

For the first half of our journey, we paralleled odoriferous convoys of "honey carts" on their way to farms. The little carters joked and larked as they led their giant horses. They might have been guiding flower-decked Rose Bowl floats rather than the contents of Tokyo's chamber pots.

As we neared our destination, we came to country where American jeeps were a comparatively rare sight. Children ran alongside us, waving their arms and crying "Banzai" and "Hurrah." I was reminded of "Liberation" greetings in the French countryside outside Paris in August, 1944.

The country beyond the town of Kasukabe was different. Farms, their pagoda roofs smothered in tall pines, formed oases in the paddy seas that stretched to the bases of distant mountains.

We turned up a dike path to one of the more prepossessing of the farms, a dozen low wooden buildings grouped around a graceful two-story pagoda-roofed house.

Keneko's friend, Iwamoto, greeted us at the gate. He was a tiny, middle-aged Japanese who wore cavalry breeches and knee-high boots. He bowed deeply to me and said in uncertain English, "Captain man welcome."

I was in uniform. This, and my beard, must have given him the impression I was an officer.

He took us into a little vine-covered Western-style frame house with sharply angled gables, set in a garden filled with pine trees, stunted palms, and flowers. I noticed beehives outside the windows. As I entered, there was a sudden flapping of wings and I looked down to see a large white rooster hopping along on a single leg. He pecked imperiously at my boots.

Keneko grinned. "That's Ondori-san—Mr. Chicken—the family pet. He seems to like you."

I fed the rooster chocolate crumbs from my pocket. He retired to a corner of the room from which he watched me with sharp eyes during the visit.

Iwamoto waved us to cane armchairs. The room was completely Western, with wooden floors, not covered with rice-straw mats. In place of a charcoal *hibachi,* there was a coal-burning potbelly stove. In one corner stood a wooden bed.

A young girl entered, carrying a tray on which was a pot of tea and a plate of cold boiled potatoes. Keneko introduced her to me as Kazuko, the youngest of Iwamoto's three daughters. She was a delightful, animated girl of about fourteen. Fresh, healthy color flooded her full cheeks. Her bright black eyes danced continually. She wore a dark blue middy over slacks.

While we drank the Scotch—Iwamoto swigging his in half tumblersful—Keneko described my studioless plight. Iwamoto was at once sympathetic. Presently he swayed to his feet and, with a sweeping gesture, proclaimed, "For Captain—all Iwamoto's farm!"

He and Keneko settled the details between them. I was to be the guest of Iwamoto and Teigo village, as long as I wished to stay. He would accept no money for lodging, food or services. When I protested to Keneko, he told me I could give them presents if I wished to.

Back in Tokyo the next day, I packed my bags and did some last minute shopping at the PX. I bought a case of Scotch, and presents of candy, food, and cosmetics. When I collected my cigarette ration, I saw bubble gum on the counter and on impulse, remembering the children I had seen, bought a large box of it.

In my absence, the floors of my new "studio" had been scrubbed, the windows cleaned and the walls decorated with sprays of blossoms. The entire family helped me get settled. Iwamoto

puffed patiently to blow up the rubber mattress for my bed. His wife, a small humble woman who spoke no English, spread soft duck-feather quilts on the bed. Takako, the middle daughter, whose full lips were always parted in wonder, was carefully laying coals in the belly stove with long chopsticks. Only four and a half feet tall, her figure was made more squat by the pregnancy that swelled her work smock. (I did not know whether I should refer to her condition, since Iwamoto had told me none of the three daughters was married.) Mitzio, the eldest daughter, who was twenty-three, looked more aristocratic than her sisters. Her face was oval, rather than round, her features more delicate, and she seemed more sophisticated. She brought in the empty whiskey bottle of yesterday, filled with boiled water, as per Keneko's instructions. (He had impressed the family with his American friend's great regard for cleanliness.)

The grandmother came in for inspection, a bent, gray-haired woman with an ancient, wise face, who tapped a cane before her. She was carrying a small bouquet of flowers for the studio.

Kazuko flashed about, helping everyone. She took turns at blowing up the mattress with her father. She rearranged the flowers in the room endlessly. When everyone had finished, she came flying in with a fresh white towel which she wrapped around my pillow. Giggling, she fed rice to Mr. Ondori-san who had taken up his billet on a bookshelf in the corner of the room.

"Ondori-san like Groth-san," she said.

I had never been so pampered in my life as I was on Iwamoto's farm. The entire family served me dinner. Because in a Japanese meal, dessert is served first, I ate pink buns that tasted like clay to me. This was followed by fish, pork, an omelette and bean-curd soup. They took turns at instructing me in the use of the chopsticks. I could see it was a struggle for them to keep straight faces at my awkward attempts to master them. Only irrepressible Kazuko tittered, however, and received a severe look from her father that caused her to beg my pardon.

In the middle of dinner that first evening, the room was plunged into darkness suddenly. Keneko had warned me that failure of electric power was a common occurrence—that it sometimes happened every evening, at least for a few minutes at a time. The family stood, beaming flashlights on my tray, while I finished dinner.

After dinner, the girls took water from a hand pump in the yard to fill the deep tub in the bathhouse. They heated it by stoking a small furnace steadily for more than an hour. After our evening whiskey, Iwamoto, bowing, told me I was to be first in the bath. The family escorted me to the bathhouse where they gave me towels and soap. Mrs. Iwamoto was sent in by her husband to test the temperature of the water. She indicated, smilingly, that it was just right.

I enjoyed soaping and scrubbing myself in the steaming neck-deep tile tub. At the crowded Correspondents' Club anything beyond a quick shower was impossible. This was the first time I had been in a tub since I had left New York.

Half an hour passed in pleasant relaxation. I searched vainly for a bath plug to let the water out. I couldn't find one. I assumed that the water had to be dipped out. The Iwamotos had politely but firmly refused to let me exert myself in any way and I felt I would be insulting their hospitality by taking the water out of the tub. So I dried myself and returned to my studio.

It was not until Keneko's next visit that I realized I had committed a grave *faux pas*. On his next trip to the farm, he took me aside and briefed me on future bathtub conduct. He explained that the single tubful of hot water was intended for use by the entire family as well as the servants. It's Japanese custom to soap yourself outside the tub, rinsing yourself with water dipped from the tub. When thoroughly clean, the bather sits in the tub and steeps. I had ruined the bath for all of the Iwamotos and their servants. They had been too polite to tell me and I had left a tub of dirtied water three nights in succession before Keneko told me the awful truth.

All the Iwamotos put me to bed. They filled the bottle of boiled water, closed the windows, placed fruit by my bed, and damped down the stove for the night. Kazuko went about spraying the room with perfume in an atomizer, despite the hoarse clucking protests of Mr. Ondori-san. The family, certain that I was comfortable, bowed out with a chorus of *"O-yasumi nasai's"* ("Good night"). The last thing I saw before I fell asleep was a huge, flat, white moon, so large that it appeared to be just outside my window.

Mr. Ondori-san awakened me at dawn with a crow so loud that I nearly fell out of bed. As if on cue, Kazuko smilingly greeted me with tea and a bright *"O-hayo, Groth-san!"* ("Good morning"). She asked my breakfast wishes. I quickly flipped through my Japanese dictionary to "soft-boiled eggs."

"Han-juku'tamagos" I told her. I wanted four-minute eggs. That made them *"Yom-pun han-juku tamagos."* To make everything perfectly clear, I made a sketch of eggs boiling in a pot over the fire. She beamed understanding.

I could hear her repeating *"Yom-pun"* to herself as she walked across the yard toward the farmhouse kitchen.

Soon the eggs arrived on a flower-embellished tray. I broke them into a cup. Though the shells were hot, the eggs were watery and looked uncooked.

Kazuko was dismayed by my disappointed expression. I thought that perhaps because of the difference between a gas range and a *hibachi,* the time must be different too. I looked up "eight minutes" in the dictionary

"Hachi-fun," I told Kazuko. She flew out of the room.

The eight-minute eggs were exactly like the four-minute ones.

This time I accompanied Kazuko into the kitchen. I had no desire to exhaust the farm's supply of fresh eggs—especially as I was keeping Ondori-san out of circulation!

Kazuko put a pan of water with two eggs on the *hibachi*. She watched her wrist watch closely.

The water had not even begun to boil over the slow *hibachi* fire when the eight minutes were up and she took the eggs from the pan. They were warm and half-raw as usual.

I gave Kazuko a quick lesson in egg cookery and from that day on, my eggs were just right.

Food was a constant problem, mainly because of our language difficulties. That same day I was served strawberries from the garden. They were large, red and succulent-looking but despite their delicious appearance they tasted sharp, acrid, not at all sweet. I left half of them in the bowl.

I assured Iwamoto I had not finished them only because I was full. He told me he was picking more for dinner.

I had occasion to enter the kitchen just before dinner. I found Kazuko with a large dish of strawberries. She was carefully soaping each individual berry with yellow laundry soap. Then I remembered Keneko's fatal instructions to the family about washing all fruits and vegetables thoroughly for their hygiene-minded guest.

While I was in the kitchen, I had noticed bluish milk in a label-less soda-pop-bottle container. When it was served to me at the table, I did not drink it. I wasn't sure it had the benefit of pasteurization and I was squeamish about the thought of the germs it might contain. Later, I was very glad I never touched the milk. One day when Iwamoto and I were out cycling, we stopped at the Kasukabe milk depot.

Buckets of milk rested on the manure littered floor of a courtyard. A naked baby was playing under a table, holding rows of unwashed pop bottles. An unusually dirty peasant woman was pouring milk into the bottles. Clouds of flies buzzed over a soiled baby diaper lying on a table in the midst of the bottles.

After breakfast the first morning, I told Iwamoto I would like to see my new neighbors and a bit of Teigo. A few minutes later he led up a huge rawboned horse that tossed his head and snorted wickedly. While Iwamoto struggled to hold him fast, I mounted him with some reservations. Unfortunately, I mounted him Western style from the left—the horse was accustomed to a Japanese right-hand mount. He immediately formed a disdainful opinion of my equestrianship.

The country whizzed past as my steed galloped over narrow paddy banks. My desperate tugging at the reins in an effort to slow him had as little effect on his tough mouth as hemp ropes would have had in holding a runaway locomotive. Farmers transplanting rice fixed in their stooped positions and stared at the apparition of bearded rider and rawboned charger, bouncing past, kicking up great clods of earth. Don Quixote and Rosinante could not have startled the peasants of La Mancha more.

I saw nothing other than flashes of shop fronts and falling bicycles as we sped through Teigo village. I pitched over the horse's neck as he ground to a sudden stop to feed on the succulent leaves of low-hanging boughs.

I was never sure whether I dragged him or he dragged me back to the farm. I selected a more manageable steed from the Iwamoto bicycle fleet. This time I had better luck, though in my effort to return the polite bows of Japanese villagers, I nearly came to grief on the narrow, slippery dike paths.

Coming back, I acquired a train of children who were never to leave me during the rest of my Teigo stay. I became their Pied Piper of Hamelin. They followed me whether I was on bicycle or on foot, no matter what direction I took or how far I went. Not only did they follow me but, as I soon discovered, they mimicked my every gesture and mannerism. They copied my exaggerated rolling gait, cleared their throats of fancied nasal drip and spat into the paddies. They hitched their trousers, lit imaginary cigarettes and puffed up their cheeks as though exhaling smoke. Even the little girls stroked imaginary beards.

I soon accepted my role as a novelty in this corner of Saitama Prefecture.

During the morning, Iwamoto had commissioned the local *daiku* ("carpenter") to make me a slanted drawing board. I found it festooned with flowers set by a window facing the road. The children who had followed me now stood at the bamboo fence at the road's edge, watching me draw. When I raised my head a few minutes later, they were in the garden feigning interest in the geese. When I looked up again, they were standing in the flower beds, frozen into awkward positions as if playing the game of "Statues." Next, they were on a line with the beehives. A problem in composition absorbed me and I forgot about them. Raising my hand to light a cigarette, I was startled to see the window covered with tiny, flattened faces. Dozens of slit eyes looked into mine.

I thought that if I gave them a present, they would return to their play. I opened the box of bubble gum and distributed pieces through the window, which I had opened. Little did I know that in that moment I had created a Frankenstein monster to plague me.

They thought the little pink blocks of gum were candy and proceeded to swallow them. I realized that bubble gum was something strange and new to their experience. I didn't know any more about blowing bubble gum than they did—it was outside my childhood experience, too—but I stood at the window chewing it with exaggerated champing of the jaws to make it pliable. My first attempts to blow bubbles were total failures.

All this time the children thought I was playing a funny game with them. They laughed and shouted. Their loud titters and yells of joy drew farmers from the paddies. Soon a crowd filled the garden and the road beyond. Finally, I achieved a bubble the size of a golf ball. This brought cheers. Everyone fell in line as I came out to distribute gum.

Perfectly charming Japanese children became bubble-gum addicts, learning to pop gum and blow bubbles the size of goldfish bowls. They spread the news of the new delight and its dispenser to boys and girls from other villages, even those beyond the horizon.

Now the yard was always filled with children. I realized I had made a grave mistake in passing out the gum, and discontinued the practice for a few days. This did not discourage the children. Droves of them advanced like Indians from point to point through the garden up to the window, trampling hedges and flowers and destroying any chance of work for me.

The first thing in the morning they were there, looking curiously at me through the window panes, as I lay in bed. I felt like Snow White with the Seven Dwarfs looking at her.

One day I decided I must be firm, even if I earned a reputation as an ogre. Out of the corner of my eye I watched them advancing from fence to garden to beehive. Suddenly, just as they neared the window, I pushed it open and screamed, "BEAT IT!" with as contorted a countenance as I could manage. I blushed with shame when they held out bouquets of rapeseed blossoms and eggs they had brought as gifts. I distributed the bubble gum and I added Hershey bars to the ration.

It became necessary for me to make weekly trips to Tokyo to replenish my supply of gum. The clerk at the candy counter of the PX told me that the "run" I was making had forced them to expand their order for it.

When I found Iwamoto rigging a support on a small tree the children had trampled, I realized the damage they were doing to the garden. I thought of all the time Iwamoto, Kazuko and others had spent, chasing them from the place—neglecting their farm tasks to do so. I apologized guiltily to Iwamoto and asked him what we should do.

He said that he would post a large sign on the gate, announcing that bubble gum would be distributed only once a day, at five o'clock and not before.

The garden gatherings ended. However, from the early hours of the morning, the road was now crowded with children. To weaken my resistance and get me to hand out the gum before five o'clock, they shouted "Hello, Bubble-san" hopefully (by this name I was now known to the countryside) and flashed mirrors into my eyes, as I tried working.

At five promptly they began to line up on the road. They cheered my appearance with salvos of *"Banzai,* Bubble Gum-san!" Each one saluted as I put a piece of gum into his eager hand, then dashed off. In a few minutes, there would not be a child in sight.

I tried to escape them by taking the bicycle out. Sometimes I actually managed to outdistance them but around the next bend in the road, I would find other groups who recognized the bearded profile of Bubble Gum-san. They would block my way over canal bridges until I dug into my pockets and passed out the gum. I had to keep my pockets filled with it.

One afternoon my supply barely met the demand. I had given out the last piece when a little girl and her two baby brothers scrambled breathlessly up the side of the dike. I rummaged in my pockets and my musette bag for a possible overlooked piece, but found nothing but a roll of Tums, the semisweet antiacid wafers for indigestion. I gave them to the three newcomers who chewed them down quickly. Their questioning eyes followed me as I guiltily rode away.

Another day I ranged into new territory, far beyond any previous journey. I stopped in a village street to see what was interesting an excited, milling crowd. In the middle, I saw two toothless old women blowing, with what seemed like their last breath, grapefruit-size bubbles.

After my ground-breaking, I feel that the Fleers Dubble Bubble Gum Company could profitably establish a depot in Saitama Prefecture to handle the demand I created.

The children were not the only ones who kept me constant company. The family, and Iwamoto in particular, treated me as though I were a week-end guest rather than a long-term liability. He was in and out of the studio at least fifty times a day. Because of his politeness and his extreme considerateness, I could not be rude, even though my work suffered because of the constant interruptions.

He would look in to see if the stove was working properly or to bring fresh cut flowers. If I looked uncomfortable sitting on a chair piled with books, he would send out for the *daiku* and have him make a new chair at a more comfortable sitting level for me. Whenever he discovered an English word that he could pronounce, he would try it out on me. If Fuji happened to emerge from behind blanketing clouds, he would drag me out to see it. No event was too slight for me to miss—the appearance of a new goldfish in the pond, a new bloom on a tree, an unusually large goose egg, anything at all.

He delighted in bringing in boxes of family photographs for me to look at. I saw hundreds of kimonoed men and women long since dead. He would ask me to pick out "Sergeant Iwamoto" in group pictures of noncommissioned officers in Manchuria. With true Japanese humility, when he showed me pictures of himself and his wife he would say, "Me—ugly man, her—ugly lady" though both of them were really quite handsome.

My presence under his roof gave Iwamoto a distinction. He was proud to introduce me to his friends. Hardly a day passed that he did not bring one or two of the shy muddy-booted farmers who bowed their shaven heads as he introduced them as "Friendos." Shortly after the introduction, Iwamoto would raise his cupped hands to his lips and make a slurping sound. This was my cue to break out the Scotch, which I never failed to do. To keep my guests away from the drawing board, where they would gape at my work, I usually set up bar at one end of the room—with bottle, glasses and cigarettes on a small table—those times I was trying to concentrate. Iwamoto usually asked for my copy of *Life's Picture History of World War II*. This would absorb the attention of the guest. They clucked their teeth as they studied photographs of Japanese triumph and defeat.

Iwamoto derived a great deal of innocent pleasure from his demonstrations of my Aerosol bomb to his friends. Evidently he imagined himself a gunner in a Zero from the aggressive way he operated it. He killed a lot of mosquitoes but he also exhausted my bomb very quickly.

I had my own Japanese visitors as well. When I was out cycling I sometimes stopped at a farm for water. My stop was always treated as an event. No matter how poor the household, they would serve me tea and cold boiled sweet potatoes. I would give them cigarettes and candy as well as the usual bubble gum. They would courteously return my visit by visiting me.

I was to regret my compliments and presents of candy to the comely gold-toothed widow of a farmer. She paid me not one but a dozen return visits, causing romantic speculation about us. She came in holiday clothes accompanied by her son, carrying apples and eggs in her *furoshiki*. She could not speak one word of English but stood in the doorway of the studio, looking at me silently, sometimes as long as an hour while I shifted from foot to foot in embarrassment, flipping through my Japanese dictionary for things to say.

I was a natural target for every student in the area who wanted to practice his English. Sometimes they wrote for appointments; sometimes they just arrived.

Tsugio Endo was in the first category. His note said, "See honorable you two o'clock come." He arrived on time, a handsome boy of sixteen accompanied by his younger brothers, all of them in blue student uniforms. They had the shy, serious look of boys applying for a job with a big corporation.

I had been under the impression that student English was fair, that we could communicate better than Iwamoto and I did. However, I quickly discovered that I was the first English-speaking person with whom they had tried to converse. My greeting of "I am happy to see you" drew blank stares and an exchange of worried looks among the three. I repeated it half a dozen times to no avail. Finally I read the stock salutation out of my Japanese-English dictionary. They replied in English, but they might as well have been speaking Japanese, for all the meaning it conveyed to me. The next few hours were verbal torture for me and surely for them. Out of our labored attempts at conversation, there were only a few facts established. I learned their ages, that the youngest of them played the violin, and that they all liked baseball—"*besu-boru*." They made it clear that they would like to visit me each afternoon to practice "*Eigo*" (English). All I got over to them, I hoped, was that I had business in Tokyo for the next few days and that meetings would be impossible for some time to come.

I thought the interview had been a miserable failure until I received a thank-you note from

Tsugio a few days later. He wrote: "Thank you very much for your many interesting and useful gossips that you told us the other day. And I had a very good time. I am very glad to see that a foreigner understand what I say and to get many things about his country also."

Saburo Yamaguchi, a twenty-one-year-old clerk in the Kasukabe tax office proved more persistent. Nothing would do but that I accompany him and his "sweetheart lady" to Tokyo to see Bing Crosby in *A Connecticut at King Arthur's Court*. (For some reason, the Japanese dropped "Yankee" from the title.)

When we got to the station, Yamaguchi immediately pointed out a pretty girl who was talking to two attentive young men on the opposite platform. This was his "sweetheart lady." She was a small girl with a cupid's bow mouth and sharply defined breasts in her pink fluffy sweater. He explained that they worked in the tax office together and to avoid embarrassment, had prearranged to join each other on the train. The two men to whom she was talking were also from their office and Yamaguchi hoped they were not going to Tokyo too.

Sako crossed to our platform when the next train pulled into the station and entered the car with the two men, passing Yamaguchi without a sign of recognition. We sat silently across from the threesome who chatted animatedly and laughed. They were obviously enjoying themselves. The train stopped every two or three miles at villages where Toyko-bound peasants poured in. Soon the small cars were crowded. Many passengers made themselves at home, stretching out at full length on the wooden benches or kicking off their *getas* (clogs) and squatting on the seats. At every platform milk in pop bottles, hard-boiled eggs, oranges and pancake-size rice crackers were sold. Hardly a pair of protruding jaws was silent. Children's dirty fingers darkened the white meat of the hard-boiled eggs they were eating.

At one village, passengers entered carrying bundles or wearing knapsacks which they parked on racks or stacked on the floor. Babies lashed on their bundle-carrying mothers' backs were crowded between back and window. Though they must have been uncomfortable in this buffer state, I never heard one cry during the entire journey. The crowd was good-natured and noisy. They gossiped with each other and showed great interest in me.

Going to Tokyo was a great occasion and they were dressed for it. Girls wore colorful dot and circle kimonos and fresh white socks fitting the foot like a glove cut with the big-toe section separate allowing for the *geta* strap. One bucolic dandy wore a belted coat, white knickers and a snap-brim hat. His socks were held on his bare shanks with Paris garters.

Yamaguchi and I violated Japanese train etiquette by rising to give our seats to a grandmother and two small children. There were many women standing on the car, some of them with babies strapped to their backs swaying over seated students who talked and joked without seeming to notice them. A Japanese man does not give his seat to a woman.

I gave some candy to the grandmother and the children who had taken our seats. A few minutes later, I noticed that the old woman was sharing a single piece with the children, passing it from mouth to mouth.

When we reached Tokyo, Sako managed to duck her two companions and joined us. At the box office of the theatre, there was an embarrassing halt as Yamaguchi borrowed the ticket money from Sako. There was no question of my paying. I can hardly say I enjoyed the film. Balconies in Tokyo theatres are much the same as those in American theatres. Boys and girls sat cheek to cheek. Peanut shells crunched under clattering *getas*. Kimonos swished noisily. The Japanese characters in the subtitles read up and down, sometimes over the faces of the actors. Everyone seemed to read the subtitles aloud.

The train ride homeward was grim. Yamaguchi and Sako were not speaking. She left the train at her stop, a village ten miles short of Kasukabe. I asked Yamaguchi why he had not taken her home. He admitted they had been quarreling. Despite the fact that this was the first time he had seen her "alone" (I didn't count because I couldn't understand Japanese), he had proposed to her. She had refused him, hence his despair. She had told him that he didn't make enough money to support a wife. I was inclined to agree with Sako when he told me that his earnings were 5,000 yen monthly, or about $15. This was hardly enough for two persons to live on. When he told me about his present dependents, I was even more convinced Sako was right. He supported his mother and his brother's wife and her two children. His father had been killed in a Tokyo air raid. His brother had been blinded in the war and was in a government hospital. Yamaguchi and his four dependents boarded at a farm near Teigo. Room and meals cost him 4,000 yen or $12 a month, leaving him 1,000 yen, or $3, for the family's other needs.

I now understood why it was necessary for him to borrow money from Sako for the tickets. Before we parted, I forced him to accept money to repay the loan.

After this, Yamaguchi and I became good friends. He decided he was out of love with Sako, but he was in love almost immediately again—at a distance, of course—with another girl in the tax office.

My existence in Lotus Land was not all rice cakes and *sake*. It began to rain about two weeks after my arrival. Heavy clouds scudded low overhead and it rained many times daily. The paddies overflowed. It was impossible to push the bicycle through the mud of the paths. The road outside my door was ankle deep in mud. The house was built flush with the ground without a basement.

I gratefully put on the GI woolen underwear I had shed so happily during the first warm days. But even the addition of heavy sweaters and tweed jacket failed to keep me warm in the penetrating dampness. My boots were always wet.

Mold began to form on everything. I scraped it from my pockets, from camera lenses and razor blades. My shoes grew beards. Every bit of leather turned green. Worst of all, my precious materials were affected. My drawing paper was always so wet that its fibre tripped the pen as I drew and spattered ink over the page.

Echelons of insects invaded the studio. Flying spiders big as a baby's hands floated between my eyes and the paper. Hundreds of tiny insects, expiring against the heated surface of the light bulb overhead, plopped softly onto my pictures, sticking to the freshly painted surface like a kind of ash. At night the frogs, multiplying by the billions, croaked in unending chorus beyond the windows. The only way I could keep warm was to get into bed or steep in a hot tub.

Diversion of any sort might have helped. But there was no one who spoke more than a few words of English for many miles around. Iwamoto and I had long since exhausted our feeble common vocabulary. There was no telephone, no corner bar, no movie house, not even a newspaper. The radio helped somewhat but all I could get was the armed-forces program from Toyko. I heard the *Tennessee Waltz* so many times that even as I write this I shudder.

I was really marooned in a damp world. Sunny Japan seemed far away. I was sustained by the thought that the rainy season could not last much longer. When Iwamoto told me that the *nyubai* or rainy reason was still a month away, I began to make plans for my departure to Southeast Asia.

My bones ached from the dampness. My muscles were always stiff and sore. One morning I had difficulty getting out of bed. Iwamoto was very concerned. He suggested a massage. I wondered why I had not thought of it myself; in New York I play handball regularly, and always follow it with a massage to work out any stiffness.

The next day a blind masseur, led by a little girl, arrived from Kasukabe. (In Eastern countries, the professional masseur is usually blind. The occupation seems to be reserved almost exclusively for the blind.) I felt immediately better. He was a good masseur. Through Iwamoto, we made an arrangement by which he would come each morning. His fee was a small one, 100 yen or 30 cents.

One morning Ondori-san, who had been suffering even more than I from the damp weather (he had developed an asthmatic cough) rooted me out of bed early with his persistent crowing. To escape his racket, I decided to take a before-breakfast constitutional. Wearing my trenchcoat and borrowing Iwamoto's umbrella, I walked to the village in a misty rain. I decided to wait for the masseur since the bus was due in a few minutes.

It arrived, discharged passengers and left. No masseur. The rain began in earnest and I stayed under the shelter of the bus depot roof. As I watched the road from Kasukabe, two figures appeared. It was the blind masseur and his little guide. As they came closer, I could see that they had no umbrellas or rain clothes. They were dripping wet, their clothes clinging to them and their bare feet raw from exposure.

When we got to the farm, I took Iwamoto aside and asked why the masseur had not come on the bus. He explained that the blind man always walked to save the fare. I was shocked. The distance from Kasukabe to Teigo was seven miles. The fare was less than five cents each way. He had walked the fourteen miles every day to save less than a dime!

It had been raining every morning for the past week and the thought of the barefooted man and the child struggling through shin-deep mud for my selfish benefit made me feel guilty.

I immediately raised his wages and gave him bus fare as well. Each day after that, I escorted them to the bus to make sure that they rode it.

One day flowed into the next on the farm. However, in mid-April came a day of tremendous excitement—the day of General Douglas MacArthur's dismissal. Kazuko came flying into the courtyard on her bicycle just before noon, her always animated face more excited than I had ever seen it. She ran to Iwamoto who was pruning a peach tree. It was a sunny day, one of the first we had had in weeks and I was working in the yard in front of the studio. I heard Kazuko hysterically repeating something in Japanese over and over to her father. Then she ran up to me.

"Shogun-Mac hima wo dasu," she cried.

Someone had turned on the radio in the main house. It was the first time I had ever heard a radio at the Iwamotos'—I hadn't even been aware they owned one.

I got the story from Iwamoto. Someone from the bicycle shop in Teigo had received the news first over the radio that morning. Kazuko's school had been closed for the day. Everyone seemed to feel General MacArthur's dismissal was a major catastrophe for Japan, comparable to a terrible earthquake.

No one worked that day. Farmers and their wives gathered about the Iwamoto radio to listen to the news broadcasts from Tokyo. There were arguments and mournful discourses in which the name "General Mac" appeared frequently. When the local paper arrived, they fought over it.

Iwamoto finally read it to them, standing on a chair from the studio.

The MacArthur regime had been a popular one. Originally, the Japanese had feared that the Occupation would be harsh. They had anticipated the victorious American Army would rape their daughters, confiscate their crops and send their sons to slave-labor camps. The leniency and good treatment of the actual Occupation had given the Japanese people new hope. The country as a whole was experiencing a rebirth. They were completely devoted to their new "Mikado" who they felt regarded them with a father's understanding. The dismissal was frightening news to them. It might mean a reversal of American Occupation policy. A change could mean harder days ahead for the Japanese.

Infected by the excitement of the farmers, I rode into Tokyo to find out more about the General's ouster, and to see the reactions there. The Correspondents' Club was in a frenzy. Dozens of newsmen argued in the bar. Others sat in their rooms, typing furiously. They were divided in their response to the lightning development. One group was entirely in accord with the President's action. They had long criticized the General's conduct of the Korean war and had blamed him for the tactics that led to disastrous retreat from the Yalu River. They were opposed by a group of devoted MacArthur admirers who felt their hero had been ungratefully treated. To them, he was the greatest living American.

At headquarters, in quartermaster supply depots, motor pools and other Tokyo military installations, there was much gloom. With the appointment of a new commanding general, shake-ups were in order. Many of the "fat cats" would have to exchange their soft Tokyo jobs for Korean foxholes. For many of them, their fears proved correct. Ridgway's new broom swept them from their desks. There was no more five-day week, golf or tennis for them.

At Teigo, the original shock gradually wore off as days passed. The new "Mikado" did not institute any drastic changes. The price of rice didn't change. Fujiyama's cone still nestled in the clouds.

The day of the MacArthur dismissal was probably the first day off Takako had had in several years. Despite her advanced pregnancy, she toiled in the fields like the others, alongside her fiancé, Shigeru Hamada. Shigeru was a thin, bespectacled boy of twenty-two from a nearby village. He and Takako were to be married at month's end. Judging from her balloon-like proportions, it would be none too soon. I dreaded the thought of her starting her labor pains during the ceremony. (I never learned, during my visit, why Shigeru and Takako were not married as soon as she found she was to become a mother.)

Takako was always the first of the household to rise. She made the fire in the stubborn *hibachi*, pumped water, fed the chickens, geese and other animals, and immediately after breakfast was out in the field, pulling heavy carts, bending over her enormous stomach as she worked in the rice fields. She took her turn at treading on the water wheel that irrigated the paddies. In addition to all this, she always seemed to be chopping up vegetables, turnips and sweet potatoes. Despite all this labor, she was always cheerful. Her smile was as bright in the evening as in the early morning. I never had seen her in any other costume than her ragged smock and slacks. I never saw her with shoes or stockings. She always wore *getas*, bare-legged.

The preparations for the wedding went on for days before the event. There was a steady whirr of sewing machines from the big house, as women sewed Takako's trousseau. Since one of the rooms in the house was to be the couple's new home, new furniture arrived by wagon from Kasukabe for it. The farm was given a face lifting—new fences were erected and trees were pruned.

New pale yellow mats of rice straw were laid on the rich, polished floors of the big house. Iwamoto made trips to Tokyo to buy delicacies for the nuptial banquet. The stock saying, "You haven't lost a daughter, you've gained a son" would be literally true for Iwamoto. He had no sons. By Japanese custom, a sonless man adopts the husband of one of his daughters at the time of the wedding. This adopted son takes his name and becomes his heir.

The morning of the big day, village women in clean white aprons and kerchiefed heads cleaned and scrubbed the big house and prepared huge quantities of food. A hairdresser imported from Tokyo dressed Takako's hair behind rice-paper panels.

As a foreigner, I was not invited to the wedding itself. However, being a denizen of the farm, I was in on the activity preceding the ceremony.

About midday, guests began to arrive. All the men were in formal frock coats and striped trousers. The women wore dress kimonos of brown, blue and black. The younger women and girls were in scarlet and pale blue kimonos. All of them rode bicycles except for important guests from Tokyo who arrived in Kasukabe's lone taxi.

Iwamoto looked very splendid in his striped trousers and tails. He was pleased when I told him he looked like Emperor Hirohito. He took his guests on a tour of the farm, the highlight, of course, being the studio with its bearded American occupant. The whiskey and *Life's* picture history got a big play.

The whole countryside stood outside the gate, watching the brilliant procession of guests parading in the garden and courtyard. A battery of cameras, including mine, clicked as Takako appeared, sumptuous in her ceremonial kimono of resplendent reds, blacks and whites. Her hair was dressed high on her head and decked with ornaments, coral and turquoise flowers and combs. I had never seen her with makeup before. She was startlingly transformed by a heavy coating of white rice powder on her face. Her eyebrows had been heavily penciled and her lips were red with lipstick. She resembled a large doll as she padded demurely through the garden. She joined Shigeru who had exchanged his work costume of Japanese military jacket and breeches for groom's dress. The local photographer fumbled beneath a dark cloth as he took first their picture, then pictures of the entire wedding party. The bride and groom posed stiffly, Takako sitting, Shigeru standing at her side. This was probably the first and only time in her life that Takako would be seated while her husband stood.

Everyone filed into the house, except me. The banquet began after the ceremony. Iwamoto thoughtfully sent one of the servants to the studio with a tray filled with wedding dainties. The villagers waited patiently at the fence. I decided to move up the hour of bubble-gum distribution. As I appeared, carrying a large box of it, the children "Banzai'd" as always.

The party lasted until evening. The guests departed, each carrying a gift box filled with cakes.

I was awakened the following morning a little before dawn by the noise of a creaking cart. Looking out the window, I was astonished to see Takako and Shigeru dressed in their work clothes on their way to the fields. The honeymoon had begun.

Despite our language barrier, I came to know the Iwamotos well in the months I spent with them. Their kitchen, which was next to my studio, was the heart of their home. I could hear them laughing and talking at meals. I never heard any quarreling. I never saw the girls in tears or sulking. They were considerate and kind to each other at all times. "Mama-san" (as I called her) and her daughters seemed completely content in their secondary status to men.

Socially, the Iwamotos were a self-sufficient family. They rarely listened to the radio; they never went to movies, or made trips to Tokyo though the city was only an hour and a half's distance. They didn't buy books or magazines. They found their relaxation and fun in each other. After dinner they spent hours gossiping and joking with each other.

They were completely unspoiled when it came to luxuries—perhaps too much so. My efforts to influence them toward adopting laborsaving electrical appliances and other necessities of Western living were failures. The four women would pore over the advertisements of these products in the *Life* magazines I brought them, exclaiming over the wonder of stoves that cooked without fires and refrigerators that held great quantities of food. But much as they admired these Western wonders, they never asked Iwamoto to buy them. I felt it was a case of their resisting change, since I knew Iwamoto was a comparatively rich man who could have afforded electric stoves and refrigerators, at least an electric iron.

When I saw Kazuko squinting over her school books in the dim kitchen, lighted by a single low-watt bulb, I realized why so many Japanese had to wear eyeglasses from an early age. Reading the complex characters in the best possible light would have strained a normal pair of eyes. One night I demonstrated the difference between their low-watt bulb and the high-watt bulb from my drawing lamp. The family exclaimed over the new brightness of the kitchen. However, they never replaced the original bulb but continued to squint in the dim light.

I was deeply conscious of their goodness to me. I am certain I was a difficult guest, perhaps the most difficult guest they could have had. Without knowing it, I must have committed dozens of *faux pas,* like the incident in the bathhouse.

I wanted to repay them in some way for their extreme considerateness. On my trips to Tokyo, I shopped carefully for unusual gifts I thought would please them. I always brought them whiskey and beer, candy and cigarettes. I brought Mama-san black pepper and white sugar which was in short supply for the Japanese.

However, my present of a can of expensive Italian cheese was a sad mistake. I opened the can and placed it on the table while they were having dinner one night. They all rose and bowed to thank me, but none of them touched it. It sat in the center of the table for several days untouched. One day I noticed it had grown a wispy mold resembling hair. I questioned Keneko about why they hadn't eaten it—at least they could have thrown it away. He told me the smell of cheese is as offensive to Japanese nostrils as the odor of rotten fish. They were too sensitive of my feelings to offend me by throwing it away.

I threw the cheese into the goat's box. I am afraid that the moldy cheese added to the egg-shells and orange peels contributed to his death soon afterwards.

My gift of a pint jar of peanut butter to Mama-san was a great success. She liked it so much that she consumed it in one sitting, eating it with a spoon as though it were a pint of ice-cream.

I dreaded my departure from these utterly kind, generous-hearted people whom I had come to love, but the time had come for me to leave them. I had one more trip to make to Korea and then I would go on to Southeast Asia.

As soon as I began to organize my belongings for the trip, a marked change came over Ondori-san. He sulked on his shelf and clucked moodily. I was out of the studio for an hour or so, and when I returned the rooster was nowhere to be seen. Then I heard a muffled noise from a suitcase which I had left open but which was now closed. I raised the top and there was Ondori-san. He looked at me with glazed eyes. Kazuko, who stood in the doorway behind me, said, "Ondori-san want go with you to America."

For a moment I had the half-mad idea of taking him with me.

The day of departure was a holiday for Teigo. All the villagers turned out. They waited about the gates during the hours it took me to pack. Takako and Kazuko had washed my shirts and pressed my clothes. The *daiku* had been working all morning to make wooden boxes for my drawings and materials. Mama-san had prepared food for the journey—enough, it seemed, to last me until I got back to the States.

I gave my gifts to the family—dress material, compacts, cosmetics and soap for the women—Zippo lighters, cartons of cigarettes and a case of whiskey for Iwamoto and his "friends." I distributed bubble gum for the last time to the clamoring children.

Iwamoto cut boughs of blossoms and tied them to the windshield of the jeep. I had to shake hands or embrace everyone. As I took my seat in the jeep beside Keneko, who had come to get me, Ondori-san flew out of the hands of Kazuko and settled in my lap. Weeping, the youngest Iwamoto daughter took him from me and held him firmly under her arm. Iwamoto leaned over the jeep side and said, "You come back some day?" I nodded.

The men and boys ran alongside the jeep as we gathered speed. The women and girls waved from the farm's gates until lost from sight. I realized, perhaps for the first time in my life, that parting was indeed "sweet sorrow."

I did not know when, if ever, I would return to this tiny corner of Saitama Prefecture but I am certain that the memory of a bearded American with a bottomless musette bag filled with bubble gum would always be kept green here.

10 · Smorgasbord

I had been hearing reports of the Jutlandia for weeks before I finally was able to visit the great hospital ship which is the Danes' unique contribution to the Korean war effort. Correspondents who had visited the floating hospital in Pusan harbor told me of its staff of world-famous surgeons and their brilliant work with the maimed and blasted. They reminisced about *smörgåsbord,* Danish beer, and pretty blonde nurses.

The dirty port of Pusan is the gate to Korea for shipping. It looked to me like any one of a dozen busy Central American harbors I had seen. The yellow-green surface of its harbor was covered with ships. Under a smoke-heavy sky, the wakes of warships, transports, and freighters crisscrossed. I saw my first Oriental junks, low wooden boats with umber and sienna sails. The shiny white of the Jutlandia, against a background of dirty gray wharves, contrasted as sharply as a cold-cream jar on a coal pile.

The 8500-ton Danish ship was moored between two American Navy hospital ships. The scene around it was active. A hospital train on tracks that went up the middle of a wide wharf was being unloaded of wounded who were being transferred to the three hospital ships. On a field adjacent to the Jutlandia's dock, Danes played a hard game of soccer. They had an eager audience of pretty nurses and bandaged men in bathrobes who watched from ship sundecks. A homeward-bound troopship moving from its slip sounded farewell blasts. The men aboard waved their hats to the convalescents on the sundecks who waved back wistfully.

Commodore Kai Hammerick, commander of the Jutlandia, reached out a friendly hand as I came up the gangplank. He was a handsome man of about sixty, with a healthy, open Scandinavian face. He looked vigorous in the dark blue, gold-braided uniform of the Royal Danish Navy. He told me I was just in time for lunch and took me into a deckwide mahogany-paneled dining saloon. Between trips to the well-laden *smörgåsbord* table for herring, fish pudding, beet salad, goat cheese and dozens of other Danish specialties, Hammerick introduced me to his staff.

Tall, handsome Tage Kjer was hobbling on a cane. He told me he had tripped on a ship's ladder while answering an alert. Kjer was head of the thoracosurgical department on the ship.

I knew Professor Eduard Busch, by reputation at least. One of the four or five finest brain surgeons in the world, he headed the neurosurgical department on the Jutlandia. He was a small balding man with heavy eyebrows. Big jolly Dr. Hans Toennesen, who bore a strong resemblance to my friend Louis Calhern, directed the general surgical staff.

Blond, blue-eyed Dr. Eric Schiodt was chief of the medical section. Hammerick introduced me to Surgeon Commander Mogens Winge, his assistant, a tall, angular Scandinavian whose pipe looked as though it had grown out of his face, it was so much a part of it.

I was on my fourth plate of *smörgåsbord* when an "alert" came. Red lights flashed wildly and bells clanged. Within a minute, the dining saloon was empty. Doctors and nurses rushed to their stations. Hammerick and I walked onto deck together to watch.

Ambulances from Pusan airport were unloading wounded on the dock. A steam winch operating from the deck lifted litters, lashed to cables, through the air and onto the three-story-high main deck. Here corpsmen guided the litters aboard and rushed the wounded men immediately to the receiving area below deck.

Hammerick invited me to accompany him on his daily tour of the wards. They were below the water line of the ship in what had been the holds in the former freight-passenger ship. They had a subterranean feeling, for they were low-ceilinged and were windowless. The first thing that struck my eye in the crowded ward was what looked like a surrealistic Christmas tree: it was a hat rack, hung with drying surgical gloves. I saw these "trees" all through the Jutlandia.

Hammerick told me that 500 workmen had worked around the clock for three months to convert the passenger liner into a hospital. In other hospital ships, beds are fixed to decks and roll with the ship. On the Jutlandia, however, the beds were attached to iron posts and set in rockers in such a manner as to resist the rolling of the ship when at sea.

"A wounded man has enough to contend with," the Commander said, "without adding seasickness to his troubles."

Hammerick stopped to speak to Carlos Hernandez, a Puerto Rican sergeant from Gaguas, Puerto Rico. Playing around his bedside was a little nine-year-old Korean girl, Hang Ok Sun. Hammerick told me she had been aboard ship for a month. The shrapnel wound in her stomach was healing nicely. She had adopted Hernandez and would climb on his bunk at least twice a day.

Hernandez grinned happily as she stroked his bandaged head. She ran to another bunk and began swinging on its railing.

"She's giving Dr. Toennesen's skin grafts a test," Hammerick laughed. He added, "I think they'll hold."

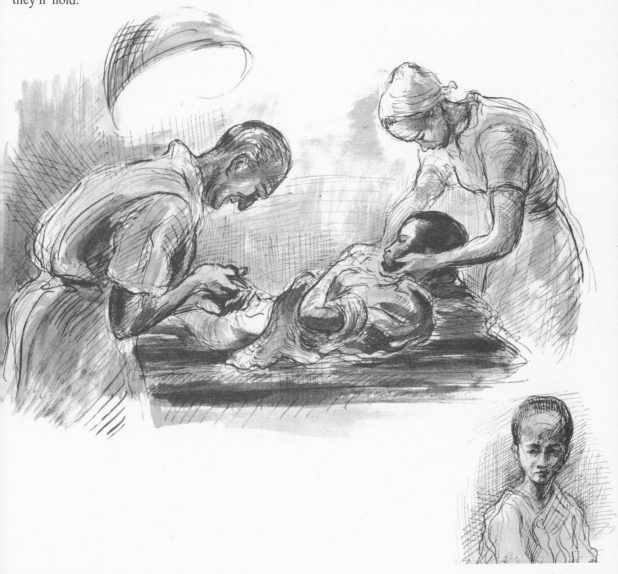

Private Clarence Parsons of Kitchener, Ontario, was visiting his old friend and fellow Canadian, Private Kenneth Hughes of Oshawa, Ontario, confined to his bunk with a leg wound. Parsons had just arrived from Canada that morning on a troopship. He had news of Hughes' mother and sister who lived with his family in Kitchener.

This was Hughes' second wound. He had no inhibitions about describing the terrors of combat with the Chinese, or the gory details of his injuries. I could see Parsons paling a bit. Finally he glanced at my correspondent's patch and asked, hopefully,

"Say, sir, do you know if there's been any talk about rotation for the Canadians?"

We didn't stop at every bed, but all the soldiers spoke to Hammerick as he passed and he had a friendly word for each one.

"Dr. Busch will take you to see some of the surgical cases tomorrow," Hammerick said. "I suppose you'd like to see your berth now." He grinned. "I'm afraid we're going to have to put you into 'solitary'—nothing personal, but we don't have much room just at the moment."

This proved to be in an isolation room in the prow of the ship, on the same level as the wards we had just visited. My gear had already been neatly stowed away. I was delighted to find that my bed was on rockers, like those I had seen in the wards.

Hammerick had given me carte blanche to wander about the ship as I wished. He told me he would be in his cabin about five if I wanted to stop in before dinner. I took a short nap, changed my clothes and went abovedeck again.

I found Hammerick in a cabin covered with photographs of his family back in Copenhagen and with colored prints of their Majesties, Frederick and Ingrid. On the bookcases were beautifully scaled ship models and souvenirs he had gathered on the trip from Denmark to Pusan, which was more than halfway around the world.

The genial Commander set out a decanter of whiskey and two glasses. I was so absorbed in what he told me about the Jutlandia I almost forgot to make the conventional sketch notes.

"As you know," Hammerick began, "my country has a record as a neutral nation. Our last war was with the Prussians back in the 19th century. Endemically, we're a peaceful country. However, we wanted to join with the other nations of the UN in the Korean action. Our government decided to send a hospital ship. In late 1950, we started to organize the expedition. I was head of the Danish Red Cross then. I've already told you how the ship was converted in three months' time into the most modern hospital ship afloat. During that same time, we selected our personnel and worked out details."

I asked Hammerick how much the ship had cost.

"It probably doesn't sound like much to you, because you are from the richest country in the world. However, if you remember that our population is less than four million—less than that of one of your large cities like Chicago or New York—you'll realize what I mean when I say this was a project in which the entire population was involved. The Jutlandia cost three and a half million or about a dollar per head. Twenty-six thousand Danes volunteered for the medical staff. There were only 100 jobs open. It broke our hearts to refuse some of those people."

I asked him about the medical equipment on the ship. This was obviously his favorite subject, next to patients, for he beamed.

He told me that the low ship-ceilings had posed a problem in the operating rooms because the powerful lamps needed over the tables would have generated an intolerable heat at the low level. American electrical experts had created a new type of high-candlepower lamp in which a system of filters removed the heat. New Swedish-constructed steel tables were fixed to the deck with special devices allowing even the most complicated operations at sea. Huge, specially constructed tanks carrying 1900 tons of fresh water had been installed.

Hammerick was proudest, however, of the ship's X-ray equipment.

"Our two portable units enable X-ray work to be done everywhere on the ship," he said.

I asked Hammerick about his background. He said he had begun his career as a young officer in the Danish navy. From there he had gone to social welfare work in London's slums.

"It was my ear that took me there," Hammerick said. "While I was serving aboard a cruiser, a white phosphorus shell exploded near me. It was an accident. The explosion burned away the back of my head and my left ear."

I looked at him in amazement: I saw what I had not noticed before—the left ear was not quite the color of the right, and the back of the Commander's head was covered with a wig.

"Let me show you my album," Hammerick said, and brought out photographs that had been taken at various stages of his "reconstruction."

Hammerick had undergone 14 operations in sixteen years. Sir Harold Gillies, the famous English plastic surgeon, had built up the back of his head with skin grafts and sculptured a new ear with skin from Hammerick's chest. That was why he had started the social work—he had been forced to stay in London during this period and months of suffering had given him a desire to help other people who were also suffering.

Looking at the pictures, it was hard for me to believe the handsome man had been so mutilated at one time. I told him so.

"I show the pictures to other badly wounded men now," Hammerick said. "It gives them hope of recovery themselves. Not so long ago an American soldier was brought aboard who had been injured in the same kind of accident as mine. He had been mangled by a phosphorus bomb. I went to see him and talked to him for quite a time about my accident and my recovery. But he would not even open his eyes during the conversation. Finally, I begged him to look at my pictures. When he did, he took heart and began to smile. You see, Mr. Groth, why I feel at home on the Jutlandia?"

Dinner was delicious. I "warmed" up with *smörgåsbord,* then ate *biksemad* (meat and potato hash with an egg on top), fruit porridge, cabbage slaw and pastry. Dr. Hans Toennesen was sitting on my right.

"By the way, your nextdoor neighbor is a patient of mine," he told me. "Would you like to pay a call on him after dinner?"

I told him I would be delighted. He told me that the patient, 2nd Lieutenant Edward Martin of the First Middlesex Regiment, had mortar wounds in his abdomen and lower back. A mortar fragment had pierced the abdomen and perforated the great intestine.

"On the first night alone, I performed three operations on Martin. I removed a large piece of his intestine. It was impossible for him still to be alive—but he was. He's put up a great struggle, yet he is so gentle and patient. He never complains, never tells us he has pain—yet we know that he has."

Only the light from a small red bulb lighted Martin's room. In that dim light, the twenty-one-year-old boy's eyes looked unusually large in his pale, wasted face. He had a high forehead and small features.

There was no mistaking the deep affection between doctor and patient. Toennesen leaned on the high railing of Martin's bunk and talked to him softly. The boy's eyes followed the surgeon's words of encouragement, balancing between anxiety and hope.

I had thought he might not want to talk about the experience that had crippled him so terribly. But he spoke freely. He had been wounded by mortar shells fired by British artillery during an uphill attack. His platoon had gained their ridge objective and he had ordered his men down into abandoned enemy rifle pits. He had been the only one standing when the shells exploded. None were to have been fired until he had sent the signal calling for them.

It had taken corpsmen three and a half hours to bring him down from the mountain. He had been carried by helicopter to a MASH unit. Afterward, he was flown to the Jutlandia.

A nurse came into the room and Toennesen asked her to bring us glasses of wine.

"You will have a glass of wine with us, my boy?" he said to Martin. The soldier nodded, smiling.

I knew from what Toennesen told me that Martin could not eat solid foods, that the surgeon encouraged him to have anything he liked—wine, beer, any liquids he wanted.

As we sipped our wine, Martin asked me about myself. He was very interested in the idea of an artist reporting the war. He asked me if I would mind bringing in some of my sketches of the Canadian, Australian and British troops I had visited. I agreed to do so if he would promise, in turn, to pose for me.

I felt guilty, showing him pictures of active, healthy men on duty and at play. He looked for a long time at one sketch of the Middlesex-Argyle football game.

"When I get back to England," Martin said, "I want to have my own farm up in the north. I hope to have a trout stream, too. I hope you and the doctor, too, will come to visit me."

I assured him that he could not keep me away—I love trout fishing. I told him about my salmon fishing in British Columbia.

"That's more sport than trout," Martin said, "I've always wanted to go to America and Canada. If I ever do get there, I won't forget the salmon."

He talked to us eagerly, but Toennesen signalled at last that he was tired and we must leave. I lay on my bunk for some time that night before I fell asleep, thinking of the boy nextdoor. I could understand Toennesen's feeling for him. Not only had his escape from death been miraculous, but he himself was an unusual human being in the degree of gentleness and tenderness he possessed. The poignancy of his hopes, especially, affected me deeply.

I spent the next day with Dr. Busch. Though I did nothing more strenuous than take notes and sketch, I was exhausted by late afternoon.

As I watched Busch and his neurosurgical team operate, I couldn't help but think of a well-oiled Notre Dame backfield—with the small balding surgeon calling the signals, of course. I watched intricate brain operations, the technicalities of which were beyond me. However, I was well aware that I was privileged in being permitted to attend an artistic performance of the first order. Dr. Busch, for all his enormous energy, worked quietly and calmly. A Marine was brought in for surgery. Dr. Busch told him that only a local anesthetic could be used in the long operation. In gentle tones he said, "You help me by lying still and I'll help you." The operation was a success and Busch complimented him with "You're a good patient." The corps-conscious soldier respectfully replied, "That's because I'm a Marine."

It was evident that Dr. Busch's staff worshipped him. He had brought his entire operating team to the Jutlandia as well as four specially trained nurses who had worked with him for eight years.

After seven hours of rigorous work, I expected the fifty-two-year-old Busch to take a few minutes' breather. Instead, he lit a pipe and invited me to see some of his "exhibits." He showed me an X-ray photograph of the brain case of a Turkish soldier. It contained bent nails, screws and

Scene in receiving below decks

other pieces of metal which had evidently been fired from a muzzle-loader. Dr. Busch had removed the metal objects from the Turk, who was still living.

"That fellow keeps nagging me for this negative," Busch chuckled. "He wants to show it off to his visitors!"

He told me he was anxious about the outcome of tomorrow's football game which he would play against the doctors from the Swedish field hospital. Reeling from the exertion of merely watching him work, I asked him how he could possibly play football after a day of operations.

"The Swedish team has beaten us three times now," he said. "And I'm going to see they don't take another game from us. It's a disgrace!"

His assistant, Dr. Kjeld Vaernet, laughed at my startled expression.

"When Busch runs out of patients," Vaernet told me, "he goes out and finds them. He can't stand waiting for them. He's got to dig up new business. He puts us in a car and spends a day at the POW camp and the children's hospital in Pusan, operating. When we get back at night, if there are new patients, we work the whole night through."

I had already heard about the children's hospital from Hammerick and was planning to visit it the next day.

I thought the loud and appreciative whistle I heard when I entered one of the wards just at supper hour was for my benefit until I turned to see a pretty nurse coming in behind me. This was Bodil Vaernet, the beautiful blonde wife of Dr. Busch's assistant, and the belle of the ship. She took the soldiers' noisy approbation in a friendly way.

The ward was alive with activity. A loud speaker blared hillbilly music (which sometimes drove the nurses to the quiet of their cabins). Ambulatory men, able to crawl out of their bunks, walked around. I saw them on the sundecks, in the PX, buying cokes, cigarettes and postcard views of the Jutlandia. They teased the nurses incessantly, just like any other soldier group.

When the supper trays arrived, I understood why one patient returning to duty had wished to have the reverse side of his dog tag engraved with "If re-wounded, please send straight to the Jutlandia."

The fare tonight was stuffed breast of veal, fried rice *Italiane,* wax bean salad, mashed potatoes, spicecake and coffee. Such a meal helped to compensate for the monotony of being bunkbound for days on end.

I was drawn to Martin's room after supper. Thinking he might like to have someone read to him, I carried with me a paper-bound copy of Dickens' *Tale of Two Cities*. He listened so raptly and stayed so quiet that at times I could not even hear his breathing and had to look at him to be sure he was still there.

"That's a good story," he said, when I put the book down after an hour or so. "Funny, I never read it myself though I like his work."

He told me about his family. His father had died when he was a small boy. I gathered they had been rather poor. Martin admitted that his principal reason for joining the Army, after he finished his education, had been to help support his mother. He told me eagerly that the Jutlandia was making a trip to Yokohama in a month. He hoped to go ashore to see Japan. Toennesen had told me that the British government had requested that he be kept aboard, since it would be dangerous to move him. The ship might make many trips before Martin could leave it. I thought of his shuttling between Pusan and Yokohama and other ports. Yet I could not feel sorry for him because he did not feel sorry for himself.

Next day I rode into Pusan in the Jutlandia's ambulance with Major Rasmus Movine, a junior surgeon, and Doctors Knud Kjaer and Lili Hjorth, another of the ship's husband-and-wife teams. We were visiting the Pusan Free Pediatric Clinic—the "Children's Hospital" to all on the ship.

We could hear children singing as we climbed to a group of buildings at the top of the hill. I understood the hospital's nickname "Happy Mountain."

Five- and six-year-olds acted out the song they were singing with exaggerated gestures. Captain Clifford G. McKeon, who met us, translated the words:

> I am very strong
> I am very happy
> I am not hungry
> I am not dying in the streets.

McKeon, who was from Perth Amboy, N. J., told me briefly about the founding of the hospital as we walked to the main building. He had conceived the idea for it one day when he found fifteen orphans begging in the streets and learned from them that they slept on sidewalks or in doorways. As we entered the building, a small boy, twisted by tuberculosis until he was no larger than a two-year-old, came running toward us.

"That's Hunch, one of the children I found begging."

"Hello, Pappa-san, number one captain," Hunch greeted him. He gave McKeon a sharp salute.

"Hunch had a profitable business in Pusan when I found him," McKeon said. "He was very well-known. Naturally, his deformity was an asset to business. Here, where there are other maimed children, he has discovered he is no longer an oddity and that he can play as much as others without being laughed at."

I had seen another small boy who had "worked" the Taegu railroad station and had gone naked even in the winter except for shoes.

Mothers were gathered about the windows of the hospital watching their children inside. McKeon told me they carried water and stoked fires and laundered sheets. Red Cross girls had decorated the ward with rabbits and elephants and other nursery characters. Papier-mâché animals peered from the shelves at the children lying or kneeling on blankets stretched on the floor. There were no cots. McKeon said they were on the way. As we passed the children, they grabbed at our hands. It was obvious that they needed affection.

Kim Wong-Ja, a four-year-old girl who had lost both her hands when her village had been shelled, was laughing at the antics of a toy mechanical donkey that wiggled his ears as he walked.

A burnt baby who had been brought in a few moments before lay in a wash basin, receiving saline solution from a glass container larger than himself. His mother crouched on the floor, watching.

The doctors were busy. McKeon asked me if I wanted to look around the grounds.

A tank truck was mounting the hill. Children spilled pellmell toward it, shouting excitedly. They leapt onto the driver as he got out of the cab of the truck, completely covering him for a minute or two. McKeon laughed at the waving arms and legs.

"They carry on like that every time they see him," he said. "He's a great favorite."

McKeon introduced me to the driver, Pfc. Edward L. Johansen of Pocatello, Idaho. The big blond water-supply soldier delivered 4900 gallons of water daily to the hospital. The clinic had no water supply of its own. Johansen, like Archie Thompson of Annapolis, Md., a Negro mess sergeant and other GI's who were nailing walls and laying tar paper on roofs, was giving all his spare time to help maintain the hospital.

I met Thompson a few minutes later in the kitchen. He was teaching Korean women hospital cookery. Outside the kitchen some sailors were erecting swings on the trench-scarred playground.

The original hospital had been housed in a small tile-roofed structure that was once a school. McKeon and his comrades had built a mess hall and outpatient clinic and had excavated under the main building to create an extra ward.

McKeon said he scrounged medical supplies, sometimes from unauthorized army sources. GI's all over Pusan gave mess rations and candy. MP's commandeered blankets and other supplies. Sailors on ships in the harbor made toys. There had only been a half dozen Korean doctors and nurses at the beginning. Now they were aided by doctors from all the UN medical installations of the area.

The little red-faced captain from Perth Amboy, who loomed so large among the children that loved him, finished his account of the kind hearts and busy hands that had aided him with, "I'm not a religious person, but the hospital has existed thus far only by faith and prayer. I must have plenty of pull upstairs. I've seen my cash balance sink to less than a nickel—but every time things look hopeless, something happens to pull us through."

As the war had moved up and down the peninsula, nearly every American company had adopted an orphan. A headquarters order put an end to this practice. Hearing of "Happy Mountain," soldiers brought their mascots to McKeon.

We happened upon a parting between a grizzled sergeant and his "adopted" boy. The child was dressed exactly like his sergeant, even to the division patch on his left shoulder. His arms held an enormous burden of candy, gum and toys, but I thought he would surely drop it at any moment, because he was looking up at the sergeant and crying as if his heart would break.

The sergeant reassured him gruffly with "That's all right, Joe. I'll be up in a few days to see you and I'll bring you a real tommy gun and a Hopalong-Cassidy outfit. Now cut out the bawlin'."

We did not linger close to this soldier-boy tableau, for from the way his grizzled face was working it looked as though the sergeant would burst into tears himself.

The gray-painted operating room was a far cry from the modern scientific perfection of the Jutlandia's. The operating table was of old Japanese manufacture and had undoubtedly seen service since the Russo-Japanese War. There was only one light bulb. Nurses tilted the shade so that the surgeons could see. The hospital's pitiful supply of instruments occupied only two glass cases. The Danish doctors worked for the most part with equipment they had brought in their bags. With Captain Kjaer doing the anesthesia, his wife and Dr. Movine operated on the children who submitted to their handling with trust and no whimpering.

In two hours I saw another minor miracle on Happy Mountain—the receiving room, which had been jammed with children when we arrived, was now clear. Dr. Movine completed his work with a skin-graft operation that took only a few minutes.

The burnt baby needed better medical attention than the limited facilities of the hospital permitted. We took him back to the ship with us. Dr. Kjaer carried him down the hill, his wife holding the bottle of saline solution. The children and mothers followed and waved good-bye to us.

We had a party aboard ship that night. There was a double celebration—it was the King's birthday and Busch had won his football game with the Swedish team.

The dining saloon was draped with Danish flags. On the captain's table, at my place, someone had placed a miniature American flag. Instead of the eternal hillbilly music on the loudspeaker, tonight we had Danish melodies. Hammerick had mentioned that the supply of Danish beer on the ship totaled 135,000 bottles. I am sure we lightened it considerably. There was wine as well.

Busch was in splendid form. As toastmaster, he proposed witty toasts—there were *"Skoals"* to the King, to the Swedes, to the patients, to me.

After we rose from the table, the floor was cleared and visiting American officers from ships in the bay, claiming the prettiest nurses immediately, led the dancing. Busch and Bodil Vaernet were the gayest couple on the dance floor.

The evening wound up with coffee and cake from the canteen.

Busch in his cabin

Dr. Kim Sae Chin   Capt. Lili Hjorth   Nurse Lee Sook Kyung   Capt. McKeon   Dr. Bak Soon Yen

Dr. Rasmus Movine

Dr. Knud Kjaer   Nurse Kim Kun Tong   Lee Poe Sik   Nurse Pak Duke Hang

109

I was leaving the next day. I had stayed up late the previous night to finish a sketch of Martin that I had promised Toennesen. I found him in the boy's room. I laid the copy of *Tale of Two Cities* on the table by Martin's bed. I was sorry I had not been able to finish reading it to him, because his pleasure in the book had increased my own affection for the story. I left the sketch of Martin with Toennesen.

I raced from stem to stern, saying good-bye to the doctors, nurses and patients I had come to know. Finally, I went to say good-bye to Hammerick.

He asked me if I would make a sketch for him in his guest book. He turned past autographs and inscriptions written by generals to his favorite page. On it an American had written "As a patient and guest on the Jutlandia, I have been completely happy and at home. Thank you, Commodore, for a wonderful 'Danish' experience."

Said Hammerick: "That, Mr. Groth, is why we came to Korea!"

Several days later I picked up a copy of the English-language paper, the *Japan News*. Midway down the page a familiar name arrested my eye. It read: "Mrs. Maude Martin arrived in Pusan yesterday, after five days and nights of plane travel from London, to visit her son, a soldier patient aboard the hospital ship Jutlandia."

11 · Pith Helmets and Curried Steak

I was lucky enough to see both the Ethiopians and the Thailanders one afternoon in a UN training area just outside Pusan. The Abyssinians were a treat for a general's eye. Spectacularly tall, handsome and regal in their pith helmets and tropical uniforms, they paraded smartly on the drill grounds, arms swinging British-style, in a manner that would have done credit to Sandhurst or West Point. They had just arrived and everything they owned was on their backs.

The Thailanders, whose camp was just up the road, were the physical opposites of the Ethiopians. The tiny yellow men wore strings of Buddhas around their necks as amulets and were the despair of American ordnance depots. They had sent more jeeps and trucks to the junk heap than enemy shells. Their favorite pastime, I shortly learned, was boxing to the accompaniment of flute and drums.

I was not prepared for the size of the Ethiopians, though I had seen enough films of the Watussi tribesmen and had watched many Negro athletes in American baseball games and track meets. All of these men were over six feet tall and their sweeping sun helmets added even more height.

I saw them first from a hill. In the distance, the blocks of men marching in a setting of tents and hills and flags reminded me of an 18th century steel engraving of the pre-battle maneuvers of a European army.

Cpl. Addmaou Tekaalign   St. Tafera Jelletu   Maj. Toorefe Teklemariam

When I came closer, I saw that they carried no rifles. Their new uniforms contrasted sharply with the weary sun- and rain-bleached uniforms of the American GIs who watched them. One GI turned to me and said, grinning, "A week on the line and their uniforms will look like ours!"

I had met Colonel Kebbede Gabre, commanding officer of the Ethiopian Expeditionary Force, on my flight from Tokyo to Pusan. The shy, attractive Colonel recognized me and came over as the men broke ranks on the field. In his very British English, he told me that the battalion I had been watching was formed from the personal guards of his Imperial Majesty, Haile Selassie. All 1500 men were volunteers. When the call for volunteers was made, Gabre said, every man in the regiment had stepped forward.

I asked him about their lack of rifles. He said they had traveled light from Africa, with only uniforms and packs, no weapons or food. They were waiting for weapons to be issued them.

"How do you think your men will do in Korea?" I asked. I always thought of Africa as a hot desert and jungle continent. I wondered how the Ethiopians would stand the extreme cold and the mountains.

"I think their experience has prepared them very well for fighting guerrillas in the Korean hill country," Gabre surprised me by saying. "They are from farm country that is always under attack by nomadic tribesmen from the mountains. They've been on many pursuing expeditions to subdue their enemies. This has certainly trained them as well as any experience could for fighting the North Koreans in the Korean mountains." He added, "They will be very useful as light infantry against infiltration and in night fighting."

He told me he had fought against the Italians to help free his homeland. He had entered Addis Ababa with the victorious Negus in 1941. Prior to being named commander of the Ethiopian Expeditionary Force, he had been Governor General of the province of Balai.

Whistles blew and the men assembled into squads for their daily conditioning exercises which proved to be very different from any other exercises I saw in Korea.

One group of men lined up in two rows, facing each other. Clasping their hands behind their backs, they butted each other, scrimmaging as in football practice. They hammered at their opponents until one in a pair was knocked from his feet. One man pushed his opponent back at least fifty feet with a powerful rush before he knocked him down. A GI whistled through his teeth in admiration. "Boy!" he exclaimed, "I'd like to see these guys up against the Chicago Bears' line."

Teams of men raced against each other in hundred-yard sprints. The winners of the heats ran in semifinals and finals. The victor was a long-limbed giant who had stripped down to his shorts, though he still wore his shirt and canvas leggings. (The leggings the Ethiopians wore were like those Americans had worn in the Spanish-American War.) I wanted to sketch him, but his commanding officer would not permit it because he was "out of uniform." He would not even tell me his name. Fearing I might think he was uncooperative, he called up several soldiers "in uniform" who stood rigidly at attention. This was exactly what I did not want. I preferred to catch the men in relaxed, unposed moments, when they were far more exciting subjects for my pencil.

These rangy Africans put me in mind of Woodruff and Borican. If Ethiopia were to send a team to the Olympics, I am sure they would score heavily in the sprints.

The exercises over, the men went to wash up for lunch. They could not use their cloth-covered *topis* for wash basins—they had not been issued steel helmets as yet—so they washed with water from "jerry" cans.

I joined the chow line. American mess sergeants served us potato salad, frankfurters, lima beans, and pineapple. The men from Africa seemed to relish the American food. One of the mess sergeants told me their food instincts were good: "They turn away from luncheon meat like good GI's."

The Baby Ruths and Hershey bars distributed after lunch disappeared immediately. It was rest period.

I wandered into the tent of Corporal Kebede Bante, thirty-one, of Merabete. He was playing a plaintive home-song on the *wahshint,* a bamboo-like pipe. Other men relaxed on cots.

Later, I watched American noncoms training the men. Mechanics showed drivers how to care for American jeeps and trucks, how to change tires, how to grease and oil them. Cooks were showing others how to prepare GI food on ovens and field stoves. They were being taught everything from the ground up. They even had to be shown how to wash their mess kits.

The Ethiopians were anxious for their guns. They gathered eagerly about American GI's and inspected their carbines and M-Is—like those they would soon be issued.

I asked an American Negro GI to pose with one of the Ethiopians, demonstrating the use of his M-I. He agreed readily, but the Ethiopians, though interested, hung back. They glanced rather nervously toward their officers. I asked one of the officers if he would persuade his men to pose with the American Negro soldier. When he hesitated I said, "You wouldn't want anyone to think that Ethiopian soldiers are forbidden to associate with American Negro soldiers, would you?"

He hastily ordered a half-dozen of his men to pose with the Negro.

Before I left, I talked with Gabre again. He admitted that his officers were sensitive about being considered Negroes by the other UN units.

"We do have Negro blood," Gabre said, "but we have many other bloods as well. You know how long ago the Israelites came to Ethiopia with the son of Sheba and Solomon. Think of the others who have come since—Egyptian and Arab traders, Portuguese Crusaders who came to aid Christian Ethiopia—we are the oldest Christian nation, by the way!—and, of course, the Italians. All this has quite changed the original African stocks."

I reminded Gabre that this was also true of the American Negro. His blood has been mixed with many others, too.

"A very good point," Gabre nodded, smiling. "I'll remember that next time I talk to my officers."

As I climbed into my jeep, I was gratified to see that the original half-dozen Ethiopians gathered around the single American Negro GI had grown to a sizable crowd. They were laughing and talking to each other, and taking turns at "sighting" the M-I.

The Thailanders were training when I entered their camp, but there was a great difference in physique between them and the men I had just left. They looked even smaller than they were— short, wide-faced men who were engaged in the same training routine as the Ethiopians. I noticed at once, however, that they were being given more intensive instruction in motor maintenance.

"They're good drivers," an American sergeant explained to me, "but when it comes time to grease the crankcase and bearings, it just sort of slips their mind. They're about as mechanical as my old lady's pet dog. The road to hell is paved with the jeeps and trucks they've wrecked because of carelessness. And that isn't the only department they got problems in. Talk to my friend over there. He'll tell you what good cooks they are!"

He gestured toward a mess sergeant who at the moment was behaving like the classic sergeant of film and comic-strip fame. His face a bright red, he waved his arms and bellowed while frightened Koreans raced about, with pots and utensils.

115

He stopped shouting when he saw me.

"Man, have we got mess problems! I thought I'd seen everything, but these Thais beat all. Do you know what they just did to me? I got me a few steaks—real steaks, the kind you serve on a platter sizzling with a side of French fries. You know what those little crackpots did with my beautiful steaks? They don't cook, of course—it's a disgrace in their country for a man to go near a cooking pot—but they gave their orders just the same to these 'gooks.' They had every one of them steaks cut into little bitty cubes and then they mixed 'em with curry and red peppers for a sauce to go on their rice." His tone expressed profound shock. "See if I ever bring one more steak to this here camp. I'm about ready to apply for my transfer!"

I could sympathize with him for I had tasted steak myself only once or twice, in Tokyo, in the last few months. Curried steak seemed like sacrilege to me, too.

Circles of men were playing *takrau,* the Thai national sport. They managed to keep a grapefruit-sized rattan ball in the air with the help of head, arms, elbows, knees and feet—any part of the body, in fact, with which they could make contact with the ball.

I was delighted when I learned that a boxing match, originally planned for the evening, had been moved up to the afternoon so that the visiting correspondent (myself) could see it. I had heard a lot about Siamese boxing, but it must be seen to be believed. It's the craziest version of a sport I have ever witnessed. Only the Harlem Globe Trotters could hold a candle, as far as pure theatric entertainment is concerned, to these Thailand pugilists.

The entire camp attended the match. The program had been mimeographed in English especially for me. The handbill shoved into my hand just before the match began announced three bouts.

The stripped contestants, bare except for loincloths, prayed in a squatting position for several seconds. Then the music began—small drums beaten by hand and flutes and pipes. The melody sounded discordant to my Western ears.

Event #1 was a five-round contest. I glanced at my handbill. The translation had been a hasty one and the idiom amused me. One of the contestants, Private Chou Bahorn, 140 pounds, was press-agented as "Tough and nimble fighter possesses terrific punch and hurtful elbow to trespass opponents with the tigery character. Always uses knee and kick to land in the solar plexus or on chins." He was fighting Corporal Chai Channa, 137 pounds, who sounded even more ferocious. "Leading kid of the Northeastern district of Korat possesses ruthless sprightly and scientific style to attack opponents surprisely with all actions by punch, reverse elbow and flying knee."

I wasn't sure just how a boxer could be "ruthless" and "sprightly" at the same time but I was willing to learn. The fighters wore gloves and the ring was roped in the conventional manner. I was anxious to observe the technique of "hurtful elbows" and "flying knees."

The build-up had been modest. Private Bahorn and I both learned (he on the jaw and "chins") how effectively a flying knee and hurtful elbow could be employed. A rapid flurry of Chai Channa's bony projections had Bahorn flat in the sand midway in the first round. He was carried away, shaking his head.

The next bout brought two foot-and-knee experts together, who miraculously weathered five rounds of dented noses and foreheads. The main bout ended with a drop kick from the foot of Sergeant Swaeng Kiath to the solar plexus of unfortunate Corporal Tem Chai. I discovered, with a sense of shock, that the music had apparently gone right on through the entire program. Fortunately, it had been drowned out by the bloodthirsty shrieks of soldier spectators.

My time at the camp was limited. I barely had time to thank Colonel Pibul Bariboon for an entertaining afternoon. I had noticed that all the small soldiers, including the boxers, wore strings of Buddhas about their necks. I wanted to know why.

117

"They're amulets," he explained. "They wear them for protection against harm."

He told me that while the religion of the Thailand soldiers is a kind of watered down Buddhism, they give credit to Buddha when they escape battle with their lives. The individual Thailand trooper feels that Buddha guides him along paths of safety.

"Several of my men talk reverently of a morning when they crossed a Korean rice field unharmed," Bariboon said. "Later in the day, Americans crossing it suffered considerable casualties. A corporal had strung two spent bullets he had found in his coat with his Buddhas—that's why they all escaped."

Whether or not Buddha is responsible for their success, the fearlessness of the 1000-man Thailand battalion is freely acknowledged by other UN troops who have had the little soldiers on their flanks.

But the presence of the Thailanders in Korea is even more important psychologically than physically, perhaps. They give lie to Communist propaganda that the war there is a war of the West against the East, of the white man against the yellow man.

12 • The Terrible Turks

Turkish attacks were now part of Korean war legend. Like the rebel war cry of the Confederate soldier, the Turks' demoniac battle cry of "Allah, Allah, Allah!" which they shriek as they rush at the enemy, has a paralyzing effect on him. They shoot and stab their way up sharp mountain slopes so rapidly that often their leading elements are caught in still-flaming napalm.

The fact that they wear the fiercest mustaches, the baggiest pants and carry the sharpest bayonets, is in perfect keeping with their reputation.

Fortune was with me again. The Turks constituted the only major UN unit in Korea I had not yet visited. Their camp was but a few miles from 25th Division headquarters at Punwon-ni, to which Red Humphries and I had jeeped madly with the correspondent pack for the great impending attack across the Han.

We had a day's grace before the attack. We arrived at 25th headquarters in the morning, had a hasty lunch, and sped to the Turks' camp.

It had snowed all that morning—the last big snow of the bitter Korean winter. Tree boughs were completely covered with the heavy fall. The snowy blanket converted the usually dismal landscape into a white dreamlike picture.

We followed a muddy trail in the snow through a narrow, twisting valley that finally opened onto a small river. Along this river the Turks had pitched their tents.

The temperature had been rising during our trip—Korea is a country of freakish weather extremes. By the time we reached the Turk camp, it was warm enough for the Anatolian soldiers to have stripped to the waist. There were half a dozen wrestling matches in progress.

119

The chest expansion of the wrestlers would have delighted Bernarr Macfadden. Their shoulders appeared to be about five feet wide and they had barrel-like torsos to go with them. Their close-cropped hair accentuated the flatness of the backs of their heads, so that their heads seemed to rise, without benefit of neck, straight out of the massive muscle of their backs and chests. Pairs grappled with one another, grunting in the lock of the unbreakable holds.

The wrestlers were completely oblivious of their grandstand referee-audience. Wrestling is so much a part of Turkish life that every male above twelve is an expert. What's more, he is vocal about it. These fellows were super-experts, judging by the noise they were making.

We watched the wrestlers in fascination for a half hour. Then Brigadier General Tahsin Yazici appeared to guide us to his small, scantily furnished tent. Straw had been spread on the ground to combat the dampness. A gasoline stove heated the General's headquarters. A small crimson Turkish flag stood out in the bleak tent, a spot of brightness on a table. I noticed an English-Turkish dictionary in juxtaposition to the inevitable field telephone.

Orderlies served us demitasse—thick Turkish coffee—and *halvah* and almonds. Yazici opened a tin of Turkish cigarettes and offered them to us. Red and I looked at each other, both remembering at the same instant that we had an acceptable present for the Turkish general in the back of our jeep. At MASH 8063, Colonel Brown had presented us with a 10-pound can of assorted nuts and a 5-pound tin of tea. We had been carrying them with us for weeks. Yazici was delighted with both nuts and tea.

There was one particularly outstanding feature in Yazici's headquarters. We were not offered liquor, as we had been at every UN camp.

My first impression of the middle-aged general was that he resembled Napoleon strikingly. His hair was combed forward, he was short and stocky.

I complimented him on his men's great reputation as fighters. I mentioned in particular their bayonet charges and the great stand they had made on the retreat from the Yalu. He protested that there had been entirely too much praise for the Turks.

"It is only their duty," he declared. "Any Turk, even those who must remain at home, would do as much. You know, of course, that any Turk who dies bravely in battle goes to heaven."

I didn't get the full impact of this until he told me that his men received no pay.

"They consider it an honor to fight for their country. Perhaps you didn't know it but no man is exempted from military service for any reason *whatsoever.*"

Red and I gasped together.

"This is not a hardship for Turkish men. The *koylus* or peasants are used to a life of extreme hardship. Our country is mountainous, our winters are cruel. As children, they run barefoot in the snow. Here, at least, they are doing what they want to do—fighting the Communists. It's almost a holiday for them," said Yazici.

There was one question that had been bothering me, but I spoke it out.

"How does it feel to be fighting alongside the Greeks, your hereditary enemy, General?"

"It is good that we fight shoulder to shoulder," he replied. "We have learned to respect each other. Our boys like each other. It's a good thing for the future, maybe one of the best things that has come out of this whole war."

I didn't say anything to this, but the General caught a quick look of slight disbelief flash between Red and me.

"I don't blame you if you are skeptical. What I have just said may sound like so much propaganda. Maybe you think my PRO told me what to say. But I can assure you I know what I am talking about—and I believe it. Mention a famous 20th-century battle in which the Turks were involved, Mr. Groth."

I quickly replied "Erzurum," and added "Smyrna."

Yazici said quietly, "I was in both those battles. I had my first command at Erzurum. I have fought the French in Syria and the British in Iraq. When I was with Atatürk, I helped drive the Greeks into the sea. I've fought a lot of different nations. And I still hold to what I say—it is good to have this friendship with our traditional enemies, the Greeks. It is also very good to have the French and English as comrades-in-arms."

Before we left his tent, Yazici showed us the flags he had received from Turkish schoolchildren. They contained messages of confidence in Turkish victory. The children had lettered them in their own blood.

"Many of our soldiers carry these flags in their bosoms when they go into battle," the General said.

He took us outside. The Turks were to cross the Han on the following day with the 25th Division. They were "rehearsing" that crossing now.

Red and I got into one of the rubber boats being used in the practice crossing. To make the test more realistic, the Turks used live ammunition. The soldiers in our boat paddled madly to beat the other boats to the opposite bank. I was soaked from head to foot by the time we reached it.

Machine guns opened as we scrambled up the bank. We dug in quickly. The guns mowed the bushes overhead. A rain of sharp twigs struck my head and sketchbook. I had no means of communicating with the men next to me. But they inscribed their names under the sketches I made of them so that I knew they were Ali Oglu Tahiralkan of Kardsu and Haeit Yesic of Ankara. Haeit Yesic was carrying a pocketful of *simitz,* out-size pretzels. He gave me a few.

Even though this was a practice, the Turks seemed to be straining like race horses at the barrier. I was amazed that some of them didn't go over the top of the bank despite the live ammunition.

Notwithstanding the realism of the drill, Yazici did not seem entirely satisfied with the performance of his men. He assured me they would be "in better form" next day, when the real attack came, and invited Red and me to go along with them. We were already committed to accompany the Americans, but I promised the small general that we would join him later in the day if possible.

Headquarters of the 25th Division at Punwon-ni was ten miles below the Han. That night generals briefed us on the battle plan. The UN forces were to cross the river near Kyongan-ni and establish bridgeheads on the north bank. In succeeding days, they would advance north in division strength. Wheeling left, they hoped to encircle Seoul, twenty-five miles downriver, within a few days. Possibly this would be the attack that would drive the enemy north of the 38th Parallel permanently.

Red and I said little to each other as we groped our way through the blacked-out camp to our billet. Our thoughts were sober. Landings are never easily accomplished: this one would be especially difficult.

We went to bed with the light of mysterious scarlet bonfires on the mountaintops flickering in our tired eyes.

13 • The Great Crossing of the Han

The rocking landscape shook snow from the trees. A stork's nest dropped at my feet. Exploding shells formed a continuous wall of fire. Reflected in the water, they added a third, molten dimension. The red dawn in the skies was paled by the blazing scarlets and seething yellows of the flame beneath.

This was H hour on the Han. This would be the final opposed crossing of the river.

I had climbed into my jeep at four that especially black morning. As we crossed the last row of hills separating us from the Han, a blast of artillery fire from a battery of 105's to the right of us momentarily lit the scene. To our left, a British battery flashed livid green. The flash of another battery down the road revealed a park of ambulances. Our jeep rocked to the steady pounding of artillery. This was the greatest concentration of artillery yet used in the Korean War. The British had joined their guns with those of the American 24th and 25th Divisions for a spectacular fire show that rivaled that I had seen at Saint-Lô in World War II.

From a hilltop back of the regiment CP at Punwon-ni, I had a dress-circle view of the fiery panorama on the opposite bank. I watched for a half hour. As the sky lightened, the planes arrived. Their bomb loads, dropping on the fire below, caused the flames to leap even higher.

Pershing tanks rumbled onto the wide stretch of snow-covered sand beach between the hills and the river. They added their own fire. Through the glasses I could see engineers—under the protecting fire of tanks—dart to the river's edge to unload sections of footbridges and rubber

125

boats from trucks. Ducks waddled down to the river. As files of tiny figures crossed the beach to board the ducks and rubber boats, the curtain of fire moved slowly up the enemy slopes opposite.

The boats, resembling beetles from a distance, moved out into the river. Enemy shells geysered the water about them. A duck, set on fire, drifted down the stream. As the shells screeched onto the beach, the rifles of soldiers flattened to the ground. When they resumed their march, some of them did not rise. Litter jeeps darted to the wounded and brought them back.

A footbridge which had nearly been completed was torn loose by the Han's angry current. Its loose end flapped against the shore. Some of the soldiers had already gained the other bank and had dug in along a crest, firing at the enemy in front of them.

I joined an infantry company that waited its turn to cross the beach. They waited, squatting in little gullies between the dunes, eyes squinted against the flame and the reflection of the rising sun on the snow. They silently watched the file of soldiers approaching the boats. When they moved out into the river, my company moved across the snow-covered sand. That is, all but one soldier who crouched near a clump of bushes that marked the border between dunes and beach.

He turned his pale face towards me and said, "My legs just won't move." After a pause, he added, "I guess I'm scared."

A shell burst blindingly near the row of tanks. I said, "You've got company, bud."

I dropped to my knees beside him as another shell screeched overhead and showered sand on us.

"What should I do, sir?" he appealed to me. "Do you think it's safe?"

I watched a litter jeep pick up two wounded men. Obviously the beach was *not* safe—no area under shellfire ever is. I could hardly tell him there was no danger.

He was waiting for an answer or reassurance of some sort. I could not help thinking his reaction was like that of Henry Fleming in *The Red Badge of Courage*. As Fleming had fled from the battle in his first shock of fear, he had suddenly thought of what his buddies would say to him that night about his loss of nerve. Briefly, I told the story to the boy.

"The rest of your outfit is out there," I said. "If you don't go, they'll know you weren't with them. When night comes, you'll have to face them. They are the men you will have to live with. What will they think of you when they find you didn't obey your orders?"

He said "Thanks a lot, sir" and ran onto the beach at the same moment a flight of dusty swallows burst from the nearby poplars.

His company was halfway across as he caught up with them. A shell burst sent them all flat against the ground. He was the last to regain his feet. When he rose, I breathed deep in relief. A moment later the company piled into boats and pushed off from shore.

I had not originally planned to cross the river under shellfire. I meant to wait until the opposite bank had been secured, and then cover the final phases of the action. I was a reporter, not a combatant. Because the scared soldier had drawn me into his problem and I had been responsible for sending him across the dangerous beach, I felt I should follow him.

Three shells dropped on the beach simultaneously. I felt there would be no more for a few moments at least so I sprinted to the edge of the river.

A group of men waited in the protective lee of trucks for their turn to board the boats. A boat had just capsized in the foaming water. A duck had rescued the soldiers in it. They huddled, shivering, about a small fire, waiting to be evacuated.

Calm engineers directed the ferrying operation. I asked one of them if he could get me across.

"You're damn right," was his terse answer. "I'm here to see that no one is left on this beach. Get in."

About midstream, a shell splashed fountains of water on us. I was already wet from the frantic paddling. We scrambled ashore. The steep bank of a hill fronted the river. We walked along, hugging it. We climbed the bank. Some of the men dropped into abandoned enemy rifle

pits. One private leapt out as quickly as if he had bounced on rubber. I looked into the hole. It held a decapitated corpse. Other enemy dead, their bodies still smoking, were scattered crazily everywhere.

Here was none of the litter of paper and possessions I had seen near dead bodies among the hedgerows and on other battlefields of World War II. In Normandy, the bodies of dead Germans and Americans had lain among scattered bits of paper, letters, newspapers, empty ration and cigarette packages, cartons, snapshots, twists of toilet paper—scraps that told, in fragments, the biographies of the dead. Here I saw nothing but an occasional rice bowl or a pair of sandals, or leaflets that had been used as toilet tissue.

There was action ahead of us somewhere to the right. We could hear the staccato of small-arms fire in the din of the barrage now shrouding the farther hills in smoke.

Companies as they landed deployed to left or right along the shore. Scrambling down the bank, I joined a platoon. Staying well below the brow of the bank, we moved silently along the river. "Return traffic" was already passing us—wounded men borne soundlessly past on litters.

I dropped into step with a lieutenant who was leading the platoon. We went several hundred yards, then turned into a small gulley that mounted the dunes. Suddenly we were under attack. Heated whisperings overhead dropped us to the ground. Men fanned out and jumped into empty rifle pits.

Machine-gun fire found us out. There was a cry of "Medics, medics!" A mortar burst near me hit two men. One was hidden by bushes. All I could see were his legs scissoring the air. A boy next to me was holding his right leg and moaning, "I've been hit, I've been hit!"

All up and down the line was the cry for "Medics." Corpsmen crawled to the screaming man in the bushes and dragged him back into the draw. He had been struck in the chest and stomach. Blood bubbled from his lips. The corpsmen placed him on a stretcher and called for clothes, jackets, blankets, anything to cover him. The jackets of the infantrymen were girded and held by belts and bandoliers. My own trenchcoat and jacket came off easily. I handed them to the corpsmen who covered the wounded man with them.

Sergeant Fred Tiedemann of Union City, N. J., cut away the pants leg and tied the thigh of the boy next to me. The boy was calm as he lay on his stomach in the snow. I smoked a cigarette with him as Tiedemann expertly bound his leg. He told me he was Private Joe Henderson, Harrisburg, Ark.

The lieutenant called for artillery support by walkie-talkie. We waited while mortar fire silenced the enemy ahead of us.

The platoon was ready to move to its next objective. Corpsmen carried away the man with the stomach and chest wounds who was now obviously dying. The lieutenant asked me if I would mind taking Private Henderson back to the beach. I agreed readily. I was not eager to go on. I was very conscious that I was of little use to the platoon. I was not adding any fire power. Besides, the ride was getting rough.

Supporting Henderson's weight on my shoulder, I served as a crutch on the slow, limping trip along the river. We were loaded onto a duck with other wounded, including the dying man from Henderson's platoon.

I rode in the jeep with Henderson to the battalion aid station which had been set up in a farmhouse on the south bank. The courtyard was jammed with wounded men still on their stretchers. Frantically busy doctors ministered to them. They were giving blood plasma to a number of soldiers. A Korean farmer and his wife stood by, obviously confused by the activity that was interrupting their accustomed pattern of life.

A doctor treated Henderson's leg on the open porch. We had become friends in our short but vital relationship. I assisted him to the jeep that was evacuating him and we said good-bye

reluctantly. On the way to the jeep, we passed a pile of bloody, discarded blankets and clothing. On top were my trench coat and jacket, which I identified by my correspondent's insignia. The soldier they had covered was dead.

It was very cold. After Henderson left, I went back and put them on again.

I returned to the north bank. During my absence, American units had moved hundreds of yards forward. They had cleared the area behind them of enemy. Only an occasional Communist shell fell now.

I crossed open fields beyond the river dunes. A lone American soldier lay sprawled stiffly across the frozen ruts of a beanfield. His outstretched hands held a pair of thick-lense glasses. I stopped to sketch him.

On the protecting slope of a railway embankment, I found a company aid station. I joined corpsmen at lunch. We sat on bloody litters and bandages to eat cold C rations.

I followed the embankment into a small town which had been taken an hour before. As I entered it, a severe explosion shook its center. I asked a passing sergeant if it was enemy shellfire.

"Naw," he drawled. "Some of the guys are tryin' to crack the safe in the town bank."

I looked into some of the houses of the captured village. On the wall of one hung an incongruous pair of pictures—a chromo of the Virgin and Child next to a portrait of Mao Tse-tung.

131

Just beyond the town, my progress toward the action, which now flared higher in the hills, was halted. A ROK private, escorting two prisoners, mistook me for an officer. With a smart salute, he surrendered his prisoners to me and left. The North Koreans, dressed in dirty quilted uniforms, kept their hands high in the air. One seemed to be having difficulty holding his up. I saw that his hand was bleeding and that the fingernails hung by bits of cuticle. Blood from his wounded hand had spotted his uniform.

For the first time since I had acquired it, I drew my .45 from its holster. I motioned my prisoners riverward on the road. I took a position to the rear of my tiny column.

The day had grown warm. It was midafternoon by now. I could hardly believe that I had stood watching the great fire show only that morning—it seemed days ago. I thought of the frightened boy on the beach, of Henderson and the other wounded man who had died, of the GI's looting the village bank. I must have been dreaming wide-awake for when I looked at my prisoners again, I discovered there were now three of them!

The newcomer was the grimmest-looking Chinese soldier I had yet seen. He was wretchedly dressed and barefoot. I tried to think of where he had joined us. Looking back over my shoulder, I saw we had passed several houses. Apparently he had been hiding in one of them. He had evidently preferred to give himself up to a bearded, unmartial-looking person like me than to a nervous-fingered GI carrying automatic weapons.

I now kept my gun leveled at the prisoners' backs, in the approved fashion. I kept it that way as we crossed the river and until I delivered them to the POW cage on the other side.

I found Red back at the press camp. We exchanged brief notes on our day's experiences before we sat down to hammer out stories on our typewriters as the other correspondents were doing.

132

Incoming reports told us that all objectives had been taken. The attack had been a smashing success. Casualties had been comparatively light. The Turks, on the right flank, had captured what was considered an almost impregnable hill fortress. I was gratified. I was sure Yazici's men would deliver.

The smiling, victorious soldiers of today's successful attack were a far cry from the grim, half-frozen snowmen I had met four months earlier. Their morale and their heads were higher now. They were confident that this was the beginning of a triumphant campaign which would force the enemy to beg for a truce.

As for me, my assignment in Korea was now finished. In a few days I would leave for Formosa and Southeast Asia. I congratulated myself that I had participated in today's attack. It was a good way to end an assignment.

14 · Fortress Formosa

All I really knew of Formosa before I visited that island was that it was the fortress home of the exiled Chiang Kai-sheks and half a million defeated Chinese Nationalist soldiers.

I found a land-poor island unable to feed its own people, much less absorb the million and a half nonfood-producing refugees and soldiers that had been dumped on it. I found a colossal military "Boys' Town" experiment in full swing—the reformation of the shattered remnants of Chiang's army into model soldiers who did not drink, smoke or wolf-call. My personal experiences with them showed me that, under this stern new regime of discipline, they had become almost Puritanical automatons—but for a purpose.

Those Chinese and Americans who spoke candidly and off the record to me despaired of the possibility of Chiang's ever leading a successful counterattack against the Chinese mainland, even if he were backed by the United States. They conceded that he could land in China with his half million soldiers and American military support, but they felt sure the invasion would die on the beaches—that the Chinese people simply would not join him.

However, under different leadership, a successful counterattack might be possible—and here I ran into the hope of the Chinese moderates, who approved of neither Mao nor Chiang: General Sun Li-jen. He enjoyed the rare reputation of being the only Chinese general who had not been defeated in a major battle.

From the air, it was hard for me to believe that the peaceful-looking green island was a military citadel. However, I began to see officers and soldiers as soon as I arrived. At the airport there were at least a dozen of the Nationalist Army's "1600 generals."

On the jeep ride to Taipeh, I saw dozens of pillboxes and roadblocks. Troops of coolie-hatted soldiers chugged past in quick-time march under the stern gaze of the Generalissimo on billboard-size portraits.

134

Taipeh was a hot, squat, dusty city of two- and three-story structures with here and there a graceful temple. Buildings were flush with the streets. Sidewalks tunneled through arcades that protected pedestrians' heads from the blistering sun and daily afternoon rains.

I had grown accustomed to the smiling, volatile Japanese. The Formosans seemed solemn-faced and inanimate by comparison. They shuffled along, carrying shallow baskets of melons and tangerines suspended from poles or sat on curbs eating slices of beef-colored watermelon without enjoyment. Shaven-headed children played silently. The children were either totally naked or wore abbreviated overalls with no seats in them. All performed their functions in public as uninhibitedly as the birds drowsing on the telephone wires above them.

The only people who seemed to be having a good time were the rich refugees from the Chinese mainland. Women and their plump husbands who wore pastel-colored Cuban-style sport shirts drove by in shiny new cars.

The city had a sleepy look. The only activity at midday when I drove through the center of town was the traffic of pedi-cabs and bicycles. Our car halted to let a string of bullock carts hauling timber and vegetables pass. Coolies without fares dozed in their parked rickshaws. The population seemed apathetic. Even the menacing glances of the omnipresent Generalissimo portrait failed to rouse them to action.

I checked into the Friends of China Club, a rambling mansion with wide porches fronting on a park. All correspondents stay there. It is only a step from National military headquarters and besides, it is the only habitable hotel in Taipeh.

On the porches, under revolving propeller-blade fans, I found American correspondents. Chinese reporters and officers from the American Military Mission playing dice and sipping iced drinks. They looked nearly as languid as the natives. It was the effect of the heat—I had only been in town for about forty-five minutes but I felt as though I had been in a steam bath the whole time.

I had barely settled myself at the Club when I started having a stream of visitors, most of them from the Nationalists' PRO. They were anxious to know what I would like to do in Formosa. They promised to fulfil as many of my requests as possible and to cooperate with me as fully as they could during my stay.

I told them I would like to do two things: interview the Chiangs and see as much as possible of the Nationalist Chinese Army. They smoothly assured me that it would be simple to arrange both these things, though they cautioned me that it might take a few days to make arrangements.

That afternoon, as I was lounging on the front porch with an orange squash in my hand, a British correspondent dropped wearily into the chair next to me. We struck up a conversation. He told me, almost at once, that he was suffering from a prolonged case of the "Taipeh Trots." A man on the other side of me said laconically, "I've got trouble the other way. I'm constipated. Have been for days."

My new British friend looked at him enviously. "Lucky devil!" he exclaimed.

He asked if I was planning to see Chiang Kai-shek. I told him of my conversation with the Nationalist PRO officers.

"I hope you've got six months or so to stick around," he said. "Unfortunately, your arrival has coincided with one of the G'imo's famous sulks. He won't be talking to any of us for a good while, I imagine."

I asked him if he had been to see Chiang yet. He shook his head.

"No, but I've got a head start on you. I've been waiting three months now."

He explained that the G'imo had it in for him and his British colleagues because of their government's recognition of Red China.

"He'll be sore at you Yanks because you didn't invite him to participate in your Japanese peace treaty."

I assured him I had a traveling schedule to keep and that I had no intention of sitting around Formosa for any great length of time.

We talked for an hour or two. I was preparing to go up to my room and change the shirt I was wearing for a cooler one when I heard someone say "Cobber!" and I turned as Warren White, big handsome Reuter's correspondent, slapped me heartily on the back. He demanded to see my room.

"If I know you, they've probably stuck you in a matchbox somewhere and you haven't even complained about it," he said.

This was the first time I had seen White since our trip to Cheechon. As we walked upstairs to my room, he told me the details of the two wounds he had received in Korea in one week. He had been sent to Taipeh to take over the Reuter's office.

"They wanted me out of Korea—were afraid of losing me!" he quipped.

He groaned in dismay when he saw the small, badly ventilated room I had been assigned to.

"You're moving out of here, Cobber," he said, "Mike James of the *New York Times* has gone to Indo-China. I'm sure his room is available. We'll get you in there."

The switch was settled in a few minutes by his persuasive talking. James's room was much larger and airier. He arranged to have a drawing board put into the room and he commandeered a couple of fans. Then he ordered me to change for dinner with him.

Before we had dinner, we toured the business section of the city. I bought a roll of Super Double X film for my camera. It cost me 75 Taipeh dollars, or about $5. Crowds of sailors and soldiers on leave wandered along the sidewalks. I commented on the solemn expressions of the natives.

White told me that they had nothing to be very happy about. In the beginning, they had hailed the Chinese Nationalists as liberators—most of them were of Chinese blood. But the Nationalists had acted like conquerors rather than liberators, appropriating all government positions and running the island as a captured colony, relegating its citizens to a secondary status. The familiar pattern of graft and corruption that had decayed Chiang's government was repeated here.

When the army arrived, the underpaid soldiers looted homes and raped local women. Formosans who had the audacity to protest were executed.

"The present reforms here haven't erased the memory of all that," White said. "Life goes on sullenly. The only hope of the people is another political arrangement that will give them kindlier masters. They'd even welcome the Japanese back."

White made me promise to keep after the Nationalist PRO's every day about the visit to the Chiangs.

I had met ECA directors on the Club's porch and they had told me the only way I could see the real Formosa would be to travel into the hills with their mobile clinics, part of their health assistance program. They arranged for me to make a trip two days after my arrival.

We dined at a Chinese restaurant he liked, an upstairs place where we sat around big tables, with cuspidors at the side into which customers spat freely. We were given damp towels to wipe our faces. I had already been warned about barber's itch at the hotel and handled my towel gingerly.

At the health center at the village of Chung Ho Hsing outside Taipeh, I sketched the sick of the neighborhood. They poured in all morning. Women with bound feet hobbled in to have their eyes washed. It seemed as though half the population suffered from trachoma. Farmer Wang Kang was brought to the station in a rickshaw, his buttocks and thighs terribly scalded. He had been arguing with his wife. When she assumed the offensive in the fight, he had stepped backward and sat in a tub of scalding water. He was naked. The villagers peered through windows and stood around the table, watching his blisters being pricked and his burns painted by a wide brush with

a pink mercurochrome-and-vaseline mixture. Afterward, he was wrapped in cellophane to keep the unguent next to his burns. His rickshaw ride home over the rutted road must have been uncomfortable. I could hear loud groans as he rode away.

I followed the mobile clinic to foothill and mountain villages, sometimes up roads so impassable that the jeep had to be abandoned and the rest of the journey made on foot.

Generally, the clinic was set up in the shade of a farm courtyard. Bridge tables held dressings and instruments. ECA emphasized, through posters, the importance of a towel for each member of the family. (One towel usually serves all members though someone in the family may be suffering from trachoma or TB.)

The clanging of hand bells summoned the sick and ailing from the surrounding countryside. Mothers brought scabby-headed babies in slings on their backs. Old people came, supporting one another. The healthy came, simply because the clinic represented an event that broke the monotony of radio- and film-less rural life. Here they met friends, gossiped, watched treatments with interest, as pigs and chickens wandered under the tables.

It was not so easy to sketch these people. Their shyness and their superstitious belief that they might lose their souls if their faces were recorded made them duck behind each other and cover their faces with their hands. When I moved toward one group with my pencil in hand, the head nurse brightly announced to them that I was a doctor. She pointed to my beard as proof. My evasive subjects became very cooperative. Perhaps they thought my pencil was an instrument with healing powers.

I followed with difficulty a midwife, a plump blue-aproned girl who propelled her bicycle with husky legs. I was many yards behind her when she reached our destination.

Most of the village was at the Chen home, thrusting their heads into doorways and windows, waiting for their newest citizen to arrive. Behind a red-checked curtain the midwife huddled with gently groaning Mrs. Chen. Peddlers, drawn by the assembly, shook rattles and sounded gongs.

I bought a bar of Camay which came to 75 cents—more than half the cost of the baby's delivery, plus pre- and postnatal care.

I was waiting on the wooden platform of a four-poster bed, drinking tea, when the baby finally was born, almost in my lap. I scampered to pass out the news. There were shouts, in Cantonese, of "It's a man child!" Grandfather Chen, who had been calmly smoking his pipe on the temple steps in philosophic fashion, came to inspect the new arrival. Father Chen, a rickshaw man, rewarded the midwife with a fast ride back to the health station. I followed, guiding her bicycle with one hand as I rode my own.

Before the end of my day with the health clinic, I knew why Formosa has been known from earliest times as "The Island of Diseases." Cholera, typhoid, malaria and dysentery have ravaged and re-ravaged it through the centuries. Today, nearly every family has one member stricken with TB. The Japanese stressed public health in the cities during their occupation, but neglected the country people. The rural health program of the ECA has done great work.

There was a message waiting for me at the Club when I returned. It said that General Chiang was still "indisposed" but that Madame Chiang would be happy to receive me the following afternoon.

However, there was one concession the PRO's asked me to make, that I allow a Brazilian photographer who wished to photograph Madame for his magazine to accompany me.

"He speaks hardly any English, Mr. Groth, so few words that it would be a great kindness if you would permit him to go with you and perhaps help him to converse with Madame," the smiling Chinese PRO told me. "This will not interfere in any way with your interview and we will be glad to arrange a second visit for you alone, later."

I could see no reason why I should refuse to take the Brazilian Luciano with me, although White was instantly disapproving when he heard about it.

"I wouldn't play journalistic wet nurse to anyone if I were you, Cobber," he advised. "It will foul up your own story."

Luciano seemed like a pleasant enough boy. As we jeeped to the Chiangs' summer home on Grass Mountain, he begged for reassurance of my help. He seemed very nervous and worried, unsure of himself. I told him sympathetically that I would do all I could.

We waited in a cool, high-ceilinged drawing room for Madame Chiang. The furniture was simple, and there were vases of flowers skilfully arranged and decorative screens. Madame Chiang entered in a few minutes. She did not look her fifty-one years. She possessed the agelessness of all beautiful women. Her slim figure could have been that of a girl in her twenties. She wore to great advantage a silk Chinese gown with a floral pattern. Her lacquer-black hair was perfectly dressed and her flawless skin, to my male eye at least, seemed untouched by makeup.

The inarticulate photographer became surprisingly eloquent. He rushed over to Madame Chiang, seized her hand and kissed it. Then, stepping back dramatically, he looked at her and said—in perfect English!—"It is true what Brazil says, what the entire world says—you are the most beautiful woman alive!"

I could have killed him with his own tripod where he stood. Madame was properly overwhelmed and blushed with pleasure. Luciano's speech had dashed the words I had meant to say to her from my mind. I mumbled some amenities which I am not sure she even heard.

Madame's male secretary and Air Force aide, attractive Chinese youths, drew the curtains to show us a magnificent aerial view of Taipeh through the great picture windows. They invited us to sit down. A servant appeared with lemonade. I had taken one sip from mine when Luciano pressed me into service as a photographer's apprentice.

I held lights for him at various angles while he posed the beaming Madame. Every time I opened my mouth to ask a question, he tossed me a flash bulb.

I felt he was trying to make amends when he asked me if I didn't want to sketch her. But I found there was a catch in this, too—he merely wanted to snap me, drawing Madame's picture. I foiled him somewhat by getting a few lines down. I was just sketching in details, when he asked me to take his picture, holding Madame's hand.

I felt the farce was getting out of hand when Madame, suddenly fatigued by the picturetaking, suggested we finish our lemonade and talk.

Desperately, I asked her about her water colors. Luciano, not giving her a chance to reply, told her that he brought her the warmest of greetings from President Vargas of Brazil. This set Madame off on a series of reminiscences about her stay in Brazil. I counted up to a thousand several times before I finally had the courage to show her my sketch. She asked if she might look through the whole sketchbook. She paused over a drawing of General Marshall which I had made at a Tokyo press conference. She spoke of him affectionately: " . . . One of the nicest and greatest men in the world today . . ." This led her to talk of America and her 1943 Washington visit when she had been cheered by both Houses of Congress.

It was Luciano's turn to glare.

Seeing that I had the upper hand for a moment, I questioned her about the role of Taipeh's women *emigrées* in the fight against Communism. She told me of the organization of the Women's Anti-Aggression League. Later, I visited the volunteer group in their quarters, the mansion of the former Japanese governor. I watched fashionably groomed women sewing bandages and puttees at a hundred sewing machines under huge pictures of Madame and of Dr. Sun Yat-sen.

When Madame Chiang had arrived from the mainland, a group of women had organized a welcome for her. Remembering the battered army that accompanied her, she ordered a plaster statue of an armless, legless soldier which was erected in the center of the stage. Madame had asked the women to contribute money for artificial limbs. Those who had come without money stripped off their jewelry—all gave generously. Enough had been collected to buy over 300 artificial arms and legs. At that moment, Madame had conceived the idea for the League. There were now 100,-000 women working everywhere on the island.

I wanted to ask her other questions, but Luciano interrupted to ask Madame if she would make a statement for the people of Brazil. When he finished asking the question, he turned to me and rather brusquely requested me to write down her reply. She complied with flowery platitudes about love and comradeship.

Graciously she signaled the interview was over. Luciano asked her to autograph a portrait of her he had bought in a camera shop. He handed me his camera bag on the way out while he waved the photograph-portrait to dry her inky signature.

He chattered enthusiastically all the way home about our "triumphant interview." I sat glumly under a pile of lights, tripod and camera cases. He was not staying at the Friends of China Club but he bounced out of the jeep and followed me up the steps. He breezily requested me to type out Madame's "message" to Brazil while he waited. After that he asked me to make a drawing of her to supplement the photographs he had taken for his magazine. Last of all I had to sketch him, also for the magazine piece. He said good-bye as though we were the best of old friends.

It was a good thing he left for Tokyo next morning because when I applied that afternoon for my second visit with Madame, I was told it would not be possible for "some months."

My disappointment was so apparent that Nationalist Army PRO officials offered to arrange immediately a trip to Tainan for me. The island's second largest city, 200 miles to the southwest, was the main training area of the Nationalist Army. They promised that I would see maneuvers on the beaches and navy installations.

I slept comfortably for the first time in Formosa on straw mats instead of sheets on a Japanese-built train. From Tainan I jeeped to the maneuver area. The beaches facing Communist China bristled with armament. Every dune concealed a pillbox filled with artillery. The sand was nettled with barbed wire. The shallow water near the beach held death for an invader: it was heavily mined. It was low tide when I arrived: wicked-looking iron rails thrust sharp points out of the surf. They would rip the bottoms from Communist landing barges, if they came. I remembered the almost impregnable German defences I had sketched along Normandy beaches after D Day in 1944. *They* had not stopped our invasion forces.

I was conducted to a high dune that contained a particularly well-fortified pillbox. The sun was so dazzling on the white sand that when I stepped onto the pillbox, I could hardly see for a moment. Everything around me seemed to be swimming. Short, thick-chested Major General Wu Ying-chi, commander of Chiang's crack division on maneuvers here, greeted me and immediately requisitioned a coolie hat for me. He stood in front of a large mapboard containing large-scale maps. The group around him hugged the shade of the mapboard. General Wu briefed us on the defence operation we were about to see. I was not the only correspondent present. A tall, lean Englishman who was filming a documentary for *The March of Time* had come along, too.

Several landing barges which appeared in the water at some distance offshore signaled the beginning of the "attack." Shells whistled as they plowed the water, short of the barges. Mines along the beach exploded, sending up fountains of sand.

General Wu told us at last that the enemy had "landed." An escorting officer took me into a rice field behind the dunes to watch counterattacking Nationalist troops. A Formosan farmer plowed stolidly behind his water buffalo, without seeming to notice the mortar battery pounding on his left or the packs of infantrymen racing along the dike on his right. The men dug in along the dunes and advanced into a graveyard where they set up their machine guns on the burial mounds. Reinforcements splashed across streams, with fixed bayonets. They rushed at barbed-wire entanglements, thrusting their bayonets into them savagely and shouting, *"Sha-ha hite!"* ("Kill them!") as they surged back and forth in mock combat.

Not all the local residents were as unperturbed as the farmer. A team of oxen galloped along the road in hysterical frenzy, their driver running alongside and attempting to calm them with a whip.

The ammunition soon ran out. General Wu told me that they had used live ammo today only because they had been assured that it would be replenished within the week. I hoped that the enemy would not choose the next few days to attack.

General Wu invited us to lunch at his headquarters just outside Tainan. The 20-foot-high ceilings of his office made it cooler than most Formosan rooms. We were handed glasses of hot water to drink, to our dismay. However, I was grateful it had been boiled; at least it was sterile. Orderlies gave us damp towels to wipe our sweaty brows. My arms smarted. Examining them, I saw that they were burnt a bright red from the sun on the beach. There were faint white blisters in places.

Lunch was served on a large round table, with bowls of rice and pork and vegetable mixture within easy reach of the diners. I was glad that Iwamoto had trained me well with the chopsticks; the General, through his interpreter, complimented me on my prowess with the sticks. He picked out especially dainty bits of meat and placed them on my plate. We ate Chinese bread, wet buns of tasteless dough. We finished with tea and the inevitable rice, which orderlies brought round in baskets. The General proved to be a "six-bowl" man.

I'm a light eater. The rich meal lay heavy on my stomach. I went to the door for a breath of air. Outside was a marvelous scene, irresistible to me as an artist. Soldiers, many of them bare from the waist up, were sitting or lying under the great spreading shade of banyan trees. They laughed and joked as they ate their lunch, crowding around rice baskets. I beckoned to *The March of Time* man. We wanted to photograph it at once. The General and his aides stopped us, however. They said that it would interfere with the afternoon's program and promised we could sketch and photograph the men at lunch the following day.

It was evident that preparations for *The March of Time* newsreelman's visit had been going on for days in advance. As we walked to the vast sun-baked squares of parade ground, surrounded by huge barracks buildings, the Englishman's face fell when he saw signs in English which designated each training group as "Machine-gun class," "Parts of the rifle class," "Log exercise," "Mortar assembly," etc. He told me he had hoped to get warm, informal pictures of the men. He hadn't wanted a posed production, at all—but this was what he was getting.

The soldiers whom we had seen relaxed at lunch a few moments before were now completely uniformed, to spiral leggings. Those attending classes sat stiffly on stools. As we approached, each group sprang to attention and then went into its act, some setting up and mock-firing mortars and machine guns. Teams of men tossed heavy logs into the air and caught them on their chests. Others strained at ropes in tug-of-war teams. Their faces were set and grim. We noticed that they continually looked at their officers out of the corners of their eyes. Their glances were fearful. One team that dropped a log seemed to "lose face" before their officers.

One group of soldiers was making rice-straw sandals. They worked in clocklike unison. The escorting officer explained that because of their shortage of clothing it was necessary for the men to make their own footgear.

I was soon bored with the automaton performance. I wanted to leave the ground. I was curious about the barracks. I was sure I would find more natural activity there or in other parts of the installation. However, whenever I made a move to go, my escorting officer politely drew my attention to some other phase of the program which he was sure would interest me.

It was almost dark by the time we were able to get away. *The March of Time* man was bitter over the thousands of feet of film he had wasted on the automatic performance of the afternoon. Just beyond the barracks, we ran into the kind of soldier activity we both had been looking for. We had been told that the Nationalists raised vegetables to supplement their bare rations. We found a number of them, in different stages of undress, in the garden behind the barracks. They were raking and weeding the plots. Some carried yokes across their shoulders from which honey buckets were suspended. There was a burst of laughter as one man raced right through the rows of vegetables in pursuit of a madly squealing pig. He landed in a bed of dirt, the pig's hind legs clasped in his arms.

Unfortunately, it was now too dark for my companion to get any pictures, or for me to sketch. We agreed that we would do it the next afternoon.

Next morning we visited the barracks. When I had peeked into the soldiers' quarters the evening before, I had seen the men lying on the long platforms where they slept, some of them naked, reading papers, wrestling, calling to one another—in short, like men in almost any other military barracks. But a startling change had taken place overnight. The billets were swept clean and scrubbed. The gear, which had been scattered about the previous evening, was arranged in neat bamboo frame packs, at the head of each mat on the sleeping platforms. Bayonets were fitted in slots. The racked rifles were aligned meticulously at the same angle. Neatly dressed men wearing caps sat rigidly on the edge of the platforms with their arms folded.

The March of Time man protested that this was not a true picture of garrison life. After an hour of argument, he convinced our escorting officers that the soldiers should look more at ease. He was finally permitted to take off a few caps and unbutton the top buttons of shirts. He posed the men in pseudo-relaxed positions from which they cautiously watched their officers. When their superiors' backs were turned, the simple peasant soldiers grinned at us. Our visit was really an event for them.

The officers became absorbed in the movie-taking—despite their stern faces and their efforts to be martinets of discipline, they were boys at heart. Unobserved, I slipped away to explore the base on my own.

Evidently we had been expected to stay in the barracks all morning. The camp was completely off guard. A company of geese waddled possessively over the parade ground. A mother goat nursed her kids under a banyan tree. Soldiers were filling a honey cart from the latrine. Others slept in the shade of trees. I looked into the soldiers' PX, a straw-thatched shack with a few bottles of beer and cider and a bowl of small peanuts on its shelves. Little clusters of men gathered around bulletin boards on which were pinned newspaper cartoons of Mao Tse-tung and Joseph Stalin being lifted sky-high by Chinese Nationalist bayonets thrust into their posteriors.

I made a few quick sketches before I was discovered by an officer. I was bold enough to ask him if I might visit the division's hospital. This took a bit of wangling but I got in.

The doctor-major in charge was the first man at the base who had spoken to me frankly. He admitted that his unit had not appeared on the parade ground at yesterday's drill because of its lack of equipment. General Wu and his officers had ordered their men to put on the best show possible for the visiting correspondents. They were anxious to create a fine impression.

145

I was shocked to hear that the division did not even have an ambulance of its own. Its one operating table was not a portable one and there were no lights for it. Aside from the ancient Japanese operating table, there was only a trunkful of old instruments. Of course there was neither an X-ray machine nor microscope. There was only a single stethoscope for the ten doctors. There was no blood bank.

I told the doctor that I could not understand how he and his colleagues worked with so little equipment.

"The worst of it is the malarial cases," he said, and showed me a half-empty jar of pellets. "This is our entire supply of atabrine. We are able to give them to the men only after they have contracted the disease. Here, I want to show you something."

He led me to a barracks room. Patients lay on platforms three tiers high—every platform covered with men.

"This month we have had four hundred and twenty-four malaria cases in the division," the doctor told me. "It's likely to get worse."

The nurses provided the final contrast to the MASH unit I had visited in Korea. They had none of the chic of the American nurses. The shapeless clothes they wore hid their charms. They could not afford hair-dos and cosmetics on their tiny salaries. In their billet there was no lingerie drying on overhead lines, no end tables burgeoning with cold-cream jars, nail polish and photographs of beaus. Their bare living quarters contained only cots. On one lay a hysterical nurse whom doctors and nurses were attempting to quiet. They had no morphine so they could not give her a shot to calm her hysteria.

General Wu met me outside his headquarters. He was in fine fettle. He rubbed his hands and beamed broadly. Through the interpreter he told me that I was to be rewarded for my patience— I was to be permitted to sketch the soldiers at lunch, while my companion could take as many pictures as he wished. No one would disturb us.

It was too good to be true—literally. The men were not under the banyan shade where they had been yesterday at lunch. Instead they had been lined in perfect rows on the parade ground, each on a small stool. They sat in the blinding heat silently and without smiles, chopsticking in unison. Our hearts sank but we sketched and photographed bravely.

After lunch we witnessed another "set-up" performance. The Chinese Nationalists are proud of all their army reforms but the one they tout most is the new system of regular pay for soldiers. On the mainland, soldiers' pay had never reached them, usually finding its way into the pockets of their officers. This had constituted the main reason for their looting. They had been forced to live off the land or starve.

Now bamboo tables were set in the sun. Soldiers stood stiffly at attention. When a man's name was called, he stepped forward to present his paybook to the paymaster who stamped it and handed him his monthly wages. This came to about 50 cents in American money, but at least the soldier received it.

In the afternoon, we again visited the garden. Whistles blew and more than 100 soldiers, wearing coolie hats, sprang into action. With the precision of Radio City Rockettes, they raked, hoed, clipped vines, and carried buckets slung on poles. All this was done with exaggerated speed, everyone moving at once. It reminded me of the old Keystone cop comedies. The pruning shears chattered like castanets. I never knew whether The March of Time documentary carried this sequence or not.

Later in the day the weary sun-beaten soldiers were marched to a Special Service show given on the stage of a bandshell. Though the actors were shaded on the stage, the soldiers squatted in precise rows, as ever in the sun. The play was a propaganda melodrama about villainous revolutionists and heroic counterrevolutionaries. Nationalist uniforms had been converted into Com-

munist uniforms by the pasting of red-paper stars on caps. To add another dimension to flat Chinese noses, black lines were painted on the ridges of actors' noses—this to accent the fact that the Reds were foreigners.

Three pretty Chinese actresses in the cast had been commissioned as lieutenants. They wore high-necked, skintight sheaths, slit thigh-high, showing the prettiest of legs. The hungry-eyed soldiers, however—unlike any other soldier audience I have ever seen—did not shout or whistle. They enjoyed the performance but did not even dare to applaud until they had been cued by the General and his officers who sat up front in the shade.

At the end of the show, the girl lieutenants refused to leave the bandshell until a covered half truck was brought alongside. As officers, they considered it undignified to be seen off stage out of uniform. I wondered at their lack of feminine vanity—their clinging costumes were infinitely more flattering than the full-cut slacks of their uniforms. Their progress across the barracks ground would have given great pleasure to the soldiers.

I was never to see the little soldiers with Formosan girls. They have no spending money for one thing. There is a language barrier for another. General Sun Li-jen, their commander-in-chief, has advised them to spend the money they do possess on food. They cannot even afford cigarettes. When I offered my pack to a group in a railway station, they refused politely and, noting an officer entering the station, moved away from me quickly.

I had never seen soldiers leading such a puritanical existence as the Chinese Nationalists did. Though they had been separated from their wives and families for a long time and obviously needed some of the ordinary pleasures as compensation, they were, in effect, forbidden women, cigarettes, liquor—even pin-ups of nude Shanghai beauties. They are separated from their officers by a tremendous social and economic gap. The officers are recruited from the educated mainland middle class. No soldier from the ranks is ever commissioned. There is no officers' training school for them. Each regiment has its political commander and is indoctrinated in the meaning of the fight against Communism. Somehow these men exist uncomplainingly through their 14-hour day, living for the moment of return to their mainland home. It seemed to me as though the spirit of Oliver Cromwell's 17th century Roundhead army had been transposed to the 20th century.

The climax of my visit in Tainan was an interview with General Sun Li-jen.

The General received me in his high-ceilinged mansion late one night. His exhausted aides were reeling to bed as I entered the large room cooled by fans that scudded overhead. This room bore the only semblance to luxury I had seen in Tainan.

The handsome, heavy-set, middle-aged general, dressed in dark-green cavalry breeches and knee boots so highly polished they reflected the glare of the light bulbs, sat comfortably in a Morris chair.

The setting was that of a Westchester home. There was a large record player and stacks of records. Bookcases were lined with leather-backed volumes. There were Chinese paintings on the

walls and life-size photographs of the Generalissimo and Madame Chiang. A bronze statue of a Manchu warrior general on a rearing horse stood on the table at the General's left. It reminded me that Sun is a cavalry man.

I mentioned the statue at once and the General smiled.

"I regret that I have no cavalry under my command," he said. "It still has a role in modern warfare—for reconnaissance and flanking movements. Look at the use the Communists have made of horses against the Americans in Northern Korea."

I told him of the sergeant I had met in Korea who wanted Missouri mules brought into the country for American use.

"They could be employed very effectively as pack animals in the mountains," the General agreed.

He was frank about the inadequacies and needs of his army.

"Our paratroopers' chutes are so rotted from age that they cannot jump. Our planes are worn out. Most of our 500 planes are grounded for lack of parts." He fingered his faded khaki shirt. "Most of us still wear the uniforms we wore in Burma. I've been wearing this shirt for four years."

I mentioned that his crack division's medical unit had no ambulance.

"We have practically no medical supplies. I wish we had a Dr. Seagrave with us now as we did in Burma. We need someone with his ability to reorganize our whole medical set-up."

I complimented him on the model behavior of his soldiers.

General Sun Li-jen smiled. "Possibly you think our discipline is hard. When we arrived in Formosa, our army was a defeated, broken one. Our men are still suffering under the weight of

152

ten years of defeat, retreat and frustration. Complete rehabilitation was necessary. We're trying to rebuild our men's minds and bodies, to give them the highest possible morale and confidence in eventual victory. The average age of our soldiers is thirty—in your army it is about twenty. Time is running out for this 'old' army. We want to use it effectively before it is too late."

I told him I had witnessed the beach maneuvers.

"That is another factor that is against us," General Sun said. "We have a crucial lack of training areas here in Formosa. Every inch of tillable ground is cultivated. We need the food too badly to interfere with the crops. That is why you see our men fighting mock battles in graveyards and on roads."

I asked the big question of the interview, "Do you think the Nationalist Army could make a successful landing on the mainland in the foreseeable future?"

"We could make the landing, with American naval help," Sun Li-jen replied, "but we could not hope to maintain ourselves there long enough for the population to come over to us unless we had a continual flow of supplies. We would need vast stock piles of ammunition, and winter clothing. Of course, modern artillery, jets and tanks would be essential. I feel we have the man power and the morale for such an operation, but we can't carry it off without American help. Your Military Mission here has already been of great help to us in streamlining our army and teaching new techniques of warfare. Just give us the weapons now and we'll do the job!"

Our serious conversation was over. The General brought out a whiskey decanter and glasses. As I sketched him, he told me of his days at Virginia Military Institute and the friends he had made in America. He talked a great deal of General Stilwell, whom he had worked with in Burma. It was very late when I closed my sketch pad, and bade him good night.

Back in Taipeh, before my departure—a group of correspondents, Chinese newspapermen and American officers—we talked of General Sun Li-jen on the porch of the Club. All had the highest regard for the General.

General
Sun Li-jen
at drill grounds

Tainan, Formosa

"If anyone could carry off a successful invasion of the mainland, it would be Sun," one of the correspondents said. "He's the man that fills the bill. The Chinese people will never rally around Chiang again—they have had enough of him and all he stands for. They might go over, though, to a leader with Sun's unimpeachable reputation, provided he made a landing and could maintain himself long enough to convince them it would be a safe move on their parts. Remember, Sun is the only undefeated Chinese General." He added softly, "A lot of people wish that Chiang would ascend to his honorable ancestors."

There was a hearty "Amen" from all in the little circle on the Club porch.

15 · Singsong Girls and Opium

I was in Hong Kong for a month before I smoked my first pipe of opium. But the preceding four weeks weren't exactly spent on the usual harbor and temple tours.

I fox-trotted with sexy singsong girls from Shanghai at the Metropole, hangout for American sailors. I lost my shirt in a fan-tan house—the only game in the world played three stories high. I dined on snake delicacies at $10 a throw. I got into a knockdown, drag-'em-out fight between British tars and merchant seamen. I watched brutal Red guards at the Chinese border mock aged nuns and missionary refugees. I spent a fascinating but sexless evening with a prostitute dressed in pedal pushers and bobby sox. And then, of course, there was the opium.

My aerial first impression of the colony of Hong Kong was of thousands of junks, their fin-shaped amethyst-colored sails dotting the yellow-green South China Sea. I wondered how many of them were innocent fishing junks and how many were smugglers, carrying contraband goods to Red China. In Formosa, Nationalist government officials had told me that most of the junks in Hong Kong waters carried contraband.

Hong Kong's main city, Victoria, is spread along a mountainside above the harbor. Its streets ran up and down the steep slopes like firemen's ladders. Its buildings sheltered two and one half million Chinese, four-fifths of them refugees from Red China, and a handful of British.

Within an hour of my landing, I was dodging double-deck London-style buses and rickshaws and sedan chairs, on Hong Kong streets. I was immediately struck by the contrast everywhere between East and West.

Red and yellow banners with wiggly Chinese characters flapped in front of signs printed in English. I stopped to look at the window display of jars of pickled snakes, dried rats, centipedes, and live baby lizards in the window of a traditional Chinese apothecary shop. Next door was a modern drugstore that sold all the standard brands of cosmetics and drugs, as well as tariff-free Chanel #5 perfume.

I stopped in front of a restaurant window in which a pair of severed bear paws beckoned to passing Chinese gourmands. Resting my sketchpad on my arm, I made quick notes of the contrasting crowd.

British officers and their wives marched past Chinese mothers nursing babies on curbs. American sailors snapped pictures of fiercely bearded Sikhs who guarded jewelry shops with shotguns. (Every gold and jewelry shop in Hong Kong employs one or two Sikh guards as protection against robbers. There were four daylight holdups during my first week.) Black-robed French priests and sallow-faced Swedish missionaries quickened their steps as they passed swivel-hipped singsong girls.

At the gate of the swanky Hong Kong Cricket Club, a pint-sized beggar woman, carrying a scabby-headed naked baby, dragged at my sleeve until I gave her a coin.

I didn't realize how hot I was until perspiration from my forehead began splashing on my sketchpad. Old China hands had warned me of Hong Kong's damp, intense heat. The English and American businessmen I passed were all wearing sports shirts and shorts. Before heading for my hotel, I bought myself a couple of the same sensible outfits.

In my air-conditioned room, I shed my sweat-soaked clothes and spent a pleasant half hour in the shower.

I expected to find the evening air cooler and more bearable. But I stepped from the hotel into a jungle sizzling with neon signs and theatre marquee lights. Titles of Hollywood gangster and cowboy films quivered in the humid air. Strings of arm-size firecrackers, announcing the opening of a new night club, ripped the night.

Kowloon, across the bay, has the same relationship to Victoria that Brooklyn has to New York. After an exotic Chinese meal that included grilled fish lips with duck sauce, sharks' fins with crab fat and stewed pigeons' eggs with fungus—an indigestible beginning for an evening—a friend and I ferried over to Kowloon.

This is the British Navy's stamping grounds. It is off limits to American sailors. On the Victoria side the same is true in reverse. My friend told me that the two navies must be kept separated for the sake of civic peace. He explained that the poorly paid British sailors cannot afford the same pleasures as the well-pocketed Americans.

We pushed our way into the noisy, crowded, smoky interior of the Red Lion, the British pub transplanted in Asia. In this famous sailor hangout the price of women and drinks had been pared to British sailor purses.

There wasn't an empty table when we entered. Her Majesty's Ship Cossack had arrived that morning. Her crew had made the Red Lion their first port of call on land. Dozens of bearded sailors contested for space at the bar with deck hands and wipers from merchant ships. The two bartenders were unable to draw the draft beer fast enough to keep their thirsty customers in brew.

You had to be pretty drunk in the Red Lion for the management to request your departure. The near-impossible happened, and we got a ringside table.

In the early part of the evening, the atmosphere was completely convivial. We joined in the general singing and clinked mugs with friendly sailors. My friend took on a huge, burly wiper at darts—a large dartboard hung at one end of the room—and won a couple of bottles of Bass for himself. While he was away from the table, I had to talk myself out of a rather embarrassing situation. An intoxicated Slavic woman with bleached blonde hair tried to join me, despite the protests of her boy friend, a sturdy deck hand. I finally persuaded her I was a Protestant minister making a survey of sin in the East.

About midnight, the tenor of the Red Lion suddenly changed. A large party of deck hands entered with girls. They were mostly dumpy, unattractive Chinese girls, not pretty enough to work the other side of the harbor. There was a White Russian who looked as though she had worked hard making her living since World War I.

The majority of men in the pub were without female companions. They resented the new party, who laughed and talked loudly and made public passes at their frumpy girl friends. A group of girl-less sailors converged on the deck hands and girls. Gradually, their comrades drifted away from the bar and ringed the table. There was a shouted insult, the sound of a chair overturning—and the battle was on. Two of the most rancorous opponents lurched towards each other and stood so close that they seemed to be roaring down each other's throats. I don't know who pushed whom, but suddenly there was a tangle of arms and legs. Mates moved in to join their companions. Non-combatants like my friend and I dove to the protection of upturned tables from which we could war-report the action without danger from flying mugs and fists.

The combatants fought in workmanlike silence except for an occasional grunt and the cracking of a split nose. Once, a broken chair violated the serenity of our foxhole. The room cleared as the action poured onto the street. The angry proprietor refused to acknowledge our neutral status. He pushed us into the street after the fighters and locked us out.

The fresher air outside sobered the warriors enough to stop sailor-against-sailor civil war. They joined forces and turned their wrath on the innocent coolies waiting for taxi fares. The sailors broke up their rickshaws, smashing one of them into the windows of the Red Lion. Warnings of a shore-patrol's imminent appearance sent them in reeling retreat to the Blue Peter several blocks away for "just one more."

As I neared my hotel in the early morning hours, I heard the hurrying high heels of night walkers echo through the arcades behind me as they converged upon me. They had spotted my Western clothes from a distance. The doorman was chasing the silk-sheathed girls from the lobby as I entered the elevator.

I visited the harbor the next morning. The docks broiled with activity. Coolies carrying backbreaking loads—square cans of tung oil, deep baskets of green and yellow vegetables, bundles of trussed red ducks—trotted past with quick short steps. I watched muscular, half-naked longshoremen, glistening with sweat, labor down gangplanks with truck-size bags of rice. They unloaded trawlers of mackerel, red sea bream and lizzard fish. Once a woman danced by me, a repulsive, dripping green fish yoked over her shoulders. I was fascinated by the grace of barefooted rickshaw coolies wearing lacquered sharp-pointed straw hats that picked up the blue of the water who slap-slapped past.

My sketchbook was filled by noon. I walked back to the hotel to make a hasty change and pick up a fresh sketchpad.

For an artist the most paintable feature of Hong Kong, perhaps, is its floating population. One hundred and fifty thousand Chinese live out their lives on sampans and junks, many of them going ashore but once—to be buried. The memorable events of existence occur on deck—birth, marriage, and propagation.

Mothers nurse babies on the polished floors of their floating homes. They cook on small charcoal braziers food bought from hawkers who paddle alongside. Pigs, dogs and chickens share sampan decks with small children. I sketched one naked baby who had a buoy tied on his back to keep him afloat in case he fell overboard. Other babies were tied with leashes that permitted them deck-wide action.

I saw at close range the junks I had seen from the plane. They looked like Spanish galleons with their high afterdecks. I examined an ancient brass swivel cannon mounted on one. This was to protect it against pirates. Others had fake gun muzzles painted on dummy portholes for the same purpose.

As I wandered slowly back to the hotel, I realized that I could spend the rest of my life here eating a different Chinese dish at every meal and still not experience them all. There were dozens of air-conditioned restaurants catering to the richer Chinese that served Canton, Peking and Szechwan specialties. There were luxurious floating restaurants where you might pick out any of a hundred different fishes, swimming in a room-size vat, and have it made into any of a dozen different dishes.

To tempt the difficult palate, there were insect delicacies such as dried cockroaches. Dried rats were another favorite. A Chinese friend said to me, "Nothing as tasty as a clean field rat."

I tried one of the striped hundred-year-old eggs I bought from a street stall. It looked and tasted much older. I decided to try a snake dinner.

The rich Chinese I had met assured me I hadn't lived, gastronomically, until I had eaten snake. I visited a snake shop I had noticed the day before. There I joined a Chinese reporter who highly recommended snake gall as being good for the circulatory system, for the scalp and eyesight. I closed my eyes and bravely swallowed the nut-size dark glob, quickly chasing it with wine. I can't say it tasted much different from my first oyster. The sensation was so strong, the flavor was lost. We stayed for a while to watch Chinese customers select live snakes the way an American would select a live lobster in a seafood restaurant.

We went on to a Chinese press banquet at which only snake was served through all five courses. I was thankful I had fortified myself well with cocktails when I saw the snakeskin soup with portions of the skin floating on its surface. The main dishes consisted of shredded snake mixed with chicken, shrimps and abalone. I self-consciously picked out the chicken and shrimp. On the pretext of making an important phone call, I left the table before the dessert course was served. We had been drinking beer with the meal but I needed whiskey. I had two double shots before I returned to my party. Needless to say, the snake dessert was lost on me!

I sobered up when I saw our publisher host count out five hundred Hong Kong dollars in payment of the check. (My share of this, back in New York, would have been $10.)

On my way home, I wondered about the ethics of Chinese chefs. I couldn't help thinking we might have been eating, without knowing it, one of the pythons that serve as ratcatchers in the city's drains.

I dropped into the Metropole Hotel one morning about eleven with two American sailors I had sketched pulling a rickshaw with their coolie as rider. (The business of reversing the roles of rider and driver is almost an initiation rite with American sailors when they hit the port. It's a common Hong Kong sight.)

The boys had told me that the Metropole was like a USO canteen with no holds barred. They could take out the girls they met here—in fact they could take them to rooms on another floor if they wished to. It could all be discreetly arranged at an accommodation desk on the floor below.

I was amazed, at that comparatively early hour—the sun was streaming through the window— to find the ballroom filled with couples who danced to a juke box or sat at tables, drinking and talking. The singsong girls who entertained the sailors wore evening gowns. They had funneled into Hong Kong from Shanghai and Canton where they had become well acquainted with free-spending Americans from ships.

We sat down at a table with a couple of pretty, slinky-hipped hostesses. One of the sailors produced a bottle of whiskey from a paper bag, and ordered setups. The girls, however, stayed with Coca Cola. None of the Oriental girls I met ever drank anything but cokes with their clients and boy friends. Eastern liquor tolerance is low. One or two drinks and an Oriental becomes over-relaxed and generous. Business girls need clear heads to bargain. They are not philanthropists.

The more petite of the two asked me to dance. She was all ready to break into a Lindy Hop, but I restrained her. My dance is the fox trot—circa 1932. We were silent until I discovered her favorite subject was American movies. The only movie stars I know personally are Sir Cedric Hardwicke and Louis Calhern, but she didn't know their names. *Her* heartbeat was Burt Lancaster, but Robert Taylor and Cary Grant were high on the list. Desperate, I invented some preposterous stories about meeting them at parties and night clubs. After the second round of *Tennessee Waltz,* I delivered her gratefully to one of the two sailors who had been tapping his foot impatiently as he watched our slow gyrations.

I left when it became obvious that the party had narrowed down to a foursome. As I said good-bye, the sailors were trying surreptitiously to pour whiskey into the girls' cokes. They winked broadly at me and wished me luck at my next "stand."

I couldn't have been in Hong Kong more than a few hours before I was aware of the under-

Hong Kong

current of Communist sympathy in the city. I had walked past one bookstore that advertised a "free" reading room several times. Finally, intrigued, I went inside.

There were two or three tables on which were arranged books, magazines and tracts at low prices within the range of coolie pockets. A bespectacled little Chinese clerk hovered over the readers, explaining characters earnestly. I helped myself to a selection of the literature on display, paid the bill and walked out.

Further down the street a Communist flag flew openly—and legally—over a restaurant. I had seen the red flag above labor-union headquarters, as well. My Chinese reporter friend had told me that two Chinese language papers followed the party line boldly. He laughed with me over some anti-American propaganda that reached the point of absurdity. It was a magazine article featuring an interview with a Chinese student recently returned from America. The student reported that his American university rented out entire dormitories as brothels.

"What would Dr. Kinsey say to that?" my friend joked.

I saw the Red Chinese face to face at the border station of Lo Wu, about twenty-five miles from Hong Kong. They lounged arrogantly against barbed-wire barricades, watching with mocking expressions the egress of burden-carrying nuns who were leaving the China they loved. A self-important Chinese WAC checked their papers on the railroad trestle bridge separating Hong Kong's New Territories from Communist China.

I offered the pudding-faced girl a cigarette. She turned away with a scornful expression, as effective as though she had spat "Capitalist!" at me. Though uniformed in shapeless faded khaki and sneakers, she was eminently more respectable than the bedraggled Chinese girl soldier I had seen hustled into a truck with other prisoners at a road junction in Korea. *She* had gratefully accepted my cigarettes and a can of C ration corned beef.

The WAC was impatient with the nuns. Old and fatigued as they were, they faltered with their answers to her staccato questions. Finally, as though oblivious of the lifetime they had spent among their adopted people in China, of their age and their extreme weariness, she gave them a surreptitious push with her short, strong hands.

A waiting group of Italian priests relieved them of their burdens. They stood under the fluttering folds of the Union Jack, one crying softly. There was very little I could do, but I wanted to do something. I bought a dozen Coca Colas from a stand in the station and carried them to the nuns. They nodded, without speaking, as they took the bottles from me.

I found Hong Kong stimulating and had no particular desire to leave until the latest possible day. However, the Chinese reporter I had by now become fast friends with, insisted that I visit Macao, on the south tip of the Pearl River estuary, forty miles away. There, he said, I would find the three cardinal pleasures, which were half-hidden in Hong Kong, in open practice—gambling, prostitution and opium smoking.

The boat on which I traveled to Macao had spiked iron grilles that guarded its upper decks from pirate attack from low-fare passengers traveling in the forward section. Armed guards eyed each passenger as he came aboard and maintained the same vigilance against each junk that neared. There were hundreds of junks within easy seeing distance. The rusty sails, patched with gray, pink and white, overlapped each other so that the horizon looked as though it were ringed with a canvas wall.

Macao could be nothing but Portuguese in influence. From the boat I could see the cobbled, winding Old World streets, the hills studded with ancient forts bristling with culverins that never fired, and—near the water's edge—Spanish baroque buildings painted in pastel colors. The blast of the ship's horn drowned out the clanging of Macao's many church bells.

Macao leads a barely tolerated existence in the jaws of the dragon. The hills of Communist China surround the little three-mile-long peninsula. Chinese flags and cannon were an ominous

note on islands at the harbor's mouth.

I was staying at the Hotel Central with a correspondent friend—the same companion I had had at the Red Lion. We had no sooner unpacked our bags when, through the open window, I heard the click of mahjong chips. We went downstairs to the gambling rooms which occupied four floors of the skyscraper hotel.

Teams of sloe-eyed girl croupiers presided over games of bird cage and fan-tan. Children were running about underfoot. Babies slept in cloth slings on their mothers' backs. The feverish play did not wake them. The rooms were large and garish: the gambling went on twenty-four hours, around the clock.

We wandered out of the hotel, down side streets, to the fan-tan houses.

Players surrounded a 20-foot-long table on the first floor and players on the second and third floors watched the table from above, looking down a well that ran from the first floor to the roof. Players on upper floors lowered their bets and collected their winnings in baskets suspended on strings.

Amid loud shouting and excitement, a grave judge-like dealer presided over the game. Bets were placed. A gong announced the beginning. Heaped on the table before the dealer was a pile of white buttons. He separated an undetermined number from the pile with a bell-shaped brass cover, then commenced drawing away four buttons at a time with a wand. The bets were made on the basis of whether there would be one, two, three or four buttons remaining at the end.

It looked very simple and I was sure that the pocketful of Macao *patacas* I had brought with me were adequate. I tried to play according to the law of averages. I saw that "four" had not come up for a number of plays so I bet on it. Three came up but, convinced that four *had* to be next, I confidently doubled my bet on four. I realized, with a shock, that my pockets were empty. I started borrowing from my friend, assuring him that I would win soon. To allay our nervousness, we bought toasted watermelon seeds and added to the number crunched underfoot. (Watermelon seeds are to a Chinese function what peanuts are to an American circus.)

I played four a dozen times more unsuccessfully, before I was convinced that this wasn't my night. A row started near the table and rifle-carrying Portuguese police poured in to break it up. The interruption was our cue to depart and save my friend's remaining *patacas*.

I was sitting in the lobby the next afternoon when someone spoke my name rather timidly. I looked up to see a remarkably appealing teen-age girl, dressed in a pink angora sweater, white pedal-pushers, pink sox and brown and white saddle-shoes. Except for her slant eyes and exotic high-boned cheeks, she might have been one of the "bobby soxers" I had seen swooning in ecstasy over "Frankie" at New York's Paramount Theatre.

She introduced herself as Cecilia. She said she had learned from the desk clerk that I was an artist and she wanted very much to have me look at her work. She, too, hoped to be an artist someday. Could I possibly come to look at her drawings?

I had no plans for the afternoon. I had been looking for an opportunity—innocent, of course—to talk to a Macao girl. This seemed too good a chance to miss.

Cecilia, despite her pedal-pushers, had come on foot. She led me through a maze of dismal, narrow streets that reminded me of parts of Greenwich Village. She was talking animatedly all the way about her favorite artist, Norman Rockwell. She told me she had "every one" of his *Saturday Evening Post* cover paintings of the last several years. She was "just crazy" about America. She asked me how I liked her costume; it, too, was modeled on the pictures she had seen of girls her own age in American magazines and American films.

I was a little shocked when Cecilia said "I live here," and stopped in front of a particularly dirty, down-at-the-heels dwelling. Naked babies, badly in need of a bath, romped and played in puddles on the cobblestone street.

Inside, an old *amah* in a stained coolie-cloth jacket and trousers was standing in a small dim room at the entrance. Several nondescript persons were huddled about the room, one of them eating rice.

A rickety staircase intruded into the room. Cecilia took my hand and led me up it. At the top, the floor was so uneven you could have put a ball on one side of the room and it would have rolled quickly to the other side. The walls looked as though they were sweating; the humidity was terrific in this old, porous house. I saw a green lizard dart across the wall as we stood for a moment outside a closed door.

"This is my room," said Cecilia, and she might have been leading me into the grand ballroom at Versailles. The room was a little larger than an American telephone booth. The bed, though narrow, dominated the room. It was actually a wooden platform, covered with faded quilts that could have taken a good laundering. A small commode—an old-fashioned washstand and pitcher—stood by the bed. On the floor was a tin bucket filled with water. My eyes went immediately to a large, naked, white chamber pot in a corner of the room beside the door. The walls were covered with the *Saturday Evening Post* covers, pasted close together perhaps in simulation of wallpaper.

Cecilia waved me primly to the bed and took a stack of art paper, covered with drawings, from under the commode. She handed them to me with a rather piteous look.

I looked through them slowly. I could not raise my eyes to hers. They were the crude drawings of an amateur, some of them copied from the Rockwell covers, others drawn from photographs of American movie stars. They were stilted, ordinary—very bad.

For once in my life, I was forced to lie to a novice artist who had asked me for my "honest opinion."

"They are very good, Cecilia," I told her. "But I think you ought to try drawing from life, too."

She asked me to show her what I meant. I made a drawing of her. She asked if she might keep it.

172

At this point, I became conscious of the noise in the house. I could hear booted feet on the stairs, strange whisperings and heavy male laughter. There was a lot of activity for so small a house. I looked at my watch and realized that it was half past eight—evening. I remembered I had a dinner engagement.

I told Cecilia that I had to go. She offered to accompany me out and get me started in the right direction towards the hotel.

At the foot of the stairs, we ran into a group of highly painted girls and Portuguese sailors and soldiers. In the small front room, a girl giggled irrepressibly on the lap of a soldier. All greeted Cecilia affectionately.

The thought struck me like a bludgeon that some of the men were waiting for Cecilia. As I walked out of the door ahead of her, I heard a man call, "Are you coming back?" and her reply, "In a few minutes."

The street had come alive. Pretty girls, most of them Chinese, sat on stools in front of the open-face, two-story houses that bordered the cobble street. Black-clad, pigtailed *amahs* sat behind them. The girls fluttered fans and called to each other. I heard Cecilia's name on all sides.

The girls sat very straight, their toes touching demurely. Potential clients window-shopped the girls' charms. Admiring little Portuguese soldiers and sailors—like those I had seen in Cecilia's house—walked slowly from one end of the street to the other, delaying as long as possible their selections.

I knew, now, that this was Macao's notorious Rua de Felicidade—"Street of Pleasure."

Cecilia left me at the end of the street. She had social obligations of her own. She told me exactly how to reach the hotel.

"Good-bye, Johnny," she said. "Please remember me just as an artist. And thank you for being kind about my drawings."

On my walks around Macao, I had smelled the sweet incense-like fragrance of opium, above odors of fish and frangipani blossoms. It came from shops and from junks and sampans. I knew that, despite the fact that opium divans were illegal, they operated in the center of the city with the connivance of corner policemen, much the same as speakeasies flourished during prohibition.

On the next to last night of our stay in Macao, a mop-haired, thin-faced Chinese with the telltale smoky eyes of the opium addict stopped us in front of our hotel. He spoke pidgin English, introducing himself as George. He was eager to guide us to a divan.

We followed, but at a distance. Avoiding patrolling police, he glided through traffic twenty feet ahead of us. He beckoned us into a tenement-type building. We descended stairs into a large basement room.

It was lighted by a bare light bulb and smokers' oil lamps which gave off an orange-colored glow. The coolies who lay on long low wooden platforms stopped smoking and paid us embarrassing attention until reassured by George that we had no police connection.

Room was made for us on the rice-straw mats that covered the platforms. The Buddha-like proprietor, his stomach rippling over his trousers—it was hot in the room—set a tray of smoking implements between us: foot-long wooden pipes, needles, tiny horn containers holding the opium, a lamp and a teapot. George presided. He dipped the needle into the dark-brown sticky fluid and roasted the drop over the flame until it bubbled and swelled, continually turning and twisting it between his fingers until it was the size of a small bead. When this grew solid, he transferred it to the bowl of a pipe. To demonstrate the smoking of it, he held the bowl inverted over the flames, sucked it deeply and quickly in a fervent panting rhythm that resulted in a steady roar like that made through a straw when a thirsty soda-drinker reaches the bottom of the glass. He prepared pipes for us and we smoked them lying on our sides, resting our heads on green porcelain blocks. A smoker requires three or four pipes to attain the languid, peaceful state. Warned by De Quincey's

173

tales of the drug's effect, I smoked only one pipe (I had a headache anyway), and enjoyed vicariously the sweet dreams of the other smokers.

There were women, one of them with her breasts exposed, in a small parlor at the end of the room. The dusty, clouded eyes of the smokers paid them scant attention. The exciting women that the opium was conjuring for them blotted out the lesser charms of those in the back room.

My companion, who is now on record as an expert, told me that opium smoking lushes occur no more frequently among smokers than liquor lushes among drinkers. An occasional pipe is a stimulant, like a shot of whiskey. Coolies carrying backbreaking burdens up mountains stop for a pipe at the roadside and renew their upward journey with fresh strength. Opium is considerably more expensive than alcoholic stimulants. The coolie cannot afford more than an occasional pipe or two. This is not apt to make a slave of him. Solitary smoking is not much fun. The pipe's effect heightens the emotions and makes a smoker conversational. He likes to meet his friends in the divan where they can talk and share their pipe dreams. It's like having a few beers at the corner bar. Television isn't missed; you project your own pictures. Several pipes smoked in rapid succession give a lift. The smoker feels strong, confident. Everyone loves him and he loves everybody else—at least these were the sensations my companion experienced. His wide-awake volubility continued long after we left the divan. The next day he took his dinner at the Lung Chi, a Macao restaurant which caters to opium smokers needing a bland diet. He enjoyed the specialty of the house—fried milk.

We left the island at night. Gasoline and rubber tires were being loaded on junks and barges by the flickering light of bonfires and lanterns, most of the work being done as always by women. That part of the Chinese population that was not gambling in the fan-tan casinos had come down to the docks for the cooler harbor breeze. They squatted amid shiny gobs of fish, gossiping and eating their suppers of noodles, pickled ginger and lotus root bought from vendors. Portuguese policemen and giant rifle-carrying Negro soldiers from East Africa strolled along the wharves watching the loading of cargo. Though much of it was obviously contraband, they did not interfere.

I got back to Hong Kong and stayed just long enough to see the completion of the new Chinese Communist bank building. It dominated the skyline, since it was two stories higher than the capitalist Hong Kong and Shanghai Bank next door—formerly the highest building in the city.

In winning the battle of altitude, the Communists lost the battle of the lions. The pair of lions resting on pedestals outside the Hong Kong and Shanghai's doors symbolized power and majesty. The Communists had commissioned a pair for their structure. When unveiled, they had been found to be smaller and less realistic than the lovely British lions. Though their abstract lines fitted beautifully into the modern design of the Communist building, they were ripped from their bases. Another pair (as far as I know) is being cast, bigger and more ferocious than their rivals, at a cost of $50,000.

Hong Kong's non-Communist residents did not regret the presence of the structure advertising Red China's power. They felt it gave them a measure of security against bombing attack should war begin. Communists would hardly do a demolition job on their architectural investment—so ran Hong Kong opinion.

During my last days, I watched life go on as usual. Bagpipers played on the lawn of the Cricket Club, painters exhibited their work. Concerts and theatricals for the next season were in the planning stage. There were cricket and tennis matches, horse races, yachting and golf.

Though the colony might seem to some observers to be living on the edge of a volcano that could erupt at any time, its members refused to die the thousand deaths of fear. They were quick to point out to American Cassandras that their prophecies of doom, made one year before my visit, had not come true. They insisted that there would always be a Hong Kong.

176

Sgt. Anverizzi
Mon Cay.

16 · Indo-China: Achilles' Heel

French Indo-China is the Achilles' heel of Southeast Asia. Throughout the East I heard, "If Indo-China goes, Thailand, Burma and Malaya will also fall to the Communists."

As I traveled through this vulnerable country, I realized how thin the French and their Viet-Nam allies had spread their defenses. Imagine that Indo-China is California: the French hold a few hundred square miles around Hanoi (San Francisco) in the north and another defense perimeter around Saigon (Los Angeles) in the south. These two areas, plus several thin strips along the coast, constitute their holdings. All the country between—roughly five-sixths of Indo-China—is held by the Viet-Minh enemy.

I visited both Hanoi and Saigon. I jeeped to Luc-Nam, a fortress on Hanoi's outer defense perimeter. I flew to Lia Chau, hemmed-in outpost on the Burmese border. And to Mon Cay, where the Foreign Legion guards the border against a half million Chinese Communists poised for an invasion that may come at any time.

Hanoi is in the center of the Red River delta, the "Rice Bowl" of the north, 75 miles upriver from the Gulf of Tonkin and 120 miles from Kwang-si Province in China. I was aware of the fact it was a city in a war zone as soon as I left the plane. Antiaircraft guns poked out of pits on the edges of the field. Tin cans were ingeniously rigged on wire as warning signals in event of attack. Our jeep's windshield was quickly covered with mud from splashing tanks and weapons carriers that passed us.

My first impression of the city itself was that it had a medieval appearance. Watch towers at either end of the mile-long bridge over the Red River bulked skyward, dominating the river like the towers of a feudal keep. Six-foot-high Senegalese cradling tommy guns guarded the bridge at fifty-foot intervals. Jagged stumps of ruins at the city's edge were mementos of its last great Viet-Minh attack. My driver reminded me that enemy-held territory was less than 35 miles from the city.

Hanoi is strictly a soldiers' town. I sat in a café the evening of my arrival, busily sketching soldiers as oddly assorted as Hannibal's Carthaginian mercenaries. They sat at tables in sidewalk cafés or stood on street corners, boldly eying clusters of Viet-Namese beauties cycling past, the trains of their colored silk tunics streaming behind them, and French women with henna hair in short swirling skirts and high wedgies.

The French had recruited their fighting men from every corner of Europe and Africa. There were Greek, Polish, Italian, Spanish and German legionnaires, most of them bearded, and distinguished by their white and red kepis. There were fierce-looking Moroccans in green turbans and red sashes. There were giant Negroes with scarified faces from Gaboon, Cameroons and the Gold Coast of Africa. French Colonial Marines in blue-black berets strolled with little Viet-Namese paratroopers. Dusty, grimy legionnaires, waving their *chapeaux de brousse* (bush hats), were arriving in trucks from delta outposts on leave. Tanned French soldiers in pin-striped "T" shirts and red pompons swaggered along the boulevards.

The cafés were doing a booming business. The soldiers danced with Viet-Namese taxi dancers to the blaring music of juke boxes and drank Algerian wine and French beer.

French PRO's billeted me in the guest house they maintained for correspondents. Like the rest of the city, the house had a French flavor. It was a Mediterranean-type villa of robin's-egg blue, set back from the tree-shaded boulevard. Sleep the first night was difficult. Pink lizards clucked amorously as they darted after each other across the ceiling of my room. Cocks announced dawn hours before morning and dogs barked through the night. Possibly I was nervous, expecting to hear the explosion of grenades and mortars in the distance. In the quiet between cock crows and dog barks, I could hear the endless honky-tonk rhapsody of juke boxes.

A good look around Hanoi next morning convinced me that the native population disliked foreigners. It was not that they were actively hostile, but that there were no friendly smiles or gestures. Even the children ignored me. Eyes evaded mine. A rickshaw man took my *piastres* in grim silence, without touching his hat with a smile like the congenial rickshaw men in Hong Kong.

I was shocked to find that a cup of bitter coffee at a café cost me ten *piastres*—fifty cents. Half a dozen golf-ball-size oranges cost 40 *piastres* or $2. I could easily chalk up Hanoi as the most expensive town I had visited on my journey halfway round the world.

There was plenty to draw however. Peasant women in cone-shaped coolie hats and dismal brown homespuns relieved by white dickies trotted along in their bare feet, their wide black trousers flapping above their bare ankles. They carried their few tattered *piastres* in poisonous-looking green and tangerine silk scarves knotted about their waists. Some carried big baskets of pomelos (the grapefruit of the East) and cabbages or soup kitchens on poles. Others squatted at sidewalk markets, selling writhing green crabs skewered on sticks and squirming mud-colored locusts and pyramids of hens in bottle-shaped wicker baskets.

The peasant women wore their black hair in coronet style, coifed tight around the head in black velvet, sausage-size tubes. This hairdress is functional; it provides a platform for the heavy loads the women carry on their heads. Their mouths are black gashes in their faces, from betel-nut chewing. A proverb of the country says: "Those who do not chew betel nut will have the white teeth of dogs."

The women of the Viet-Namese bourgeoisie offered a graceful contrast to their peasant sisters. They clattered by daintily on wooden clogs. Their costumes were the delicate shades of Jordan almonds—over wide silk trousers, they wore slit, ankle-length tunics in pale pink, green, yellow and orange silk. Their rich black hair poured down their backs, caught by barrettes. Again the Gallic note—some of the women carried parasols and long loaves of French bread. This seemed perfectly appropriate against the background of the full-blown Gothic cathedral that stood at the center of the city. The architecture as a whole was French in spirit and the sidewalk cafés and Citroen cars reminded me of Paris.

Dinner that night was memorable for me. The entrée was a tiny *béccasine*—sandpiper-like birds—roasted with their craws still filled with insects. They tasted like liver—and I've never liked liver. I eked out the meal with pieces of the yard-long French bread and red wine.

I was waiting for an opportunity to go on a combat mission. Captain André Wastin, PRO officer, a charming Frenchman from Rouen, saw to it that my schedule was filled with visits to outposts of the perimeter.

He was my escort officer on all these trips. The French had hedged Hanoi with a bristling ring of concrete pillboxes, barbed wire, pointed bamboo stakes, even broken glass—anything to stop a barefooted enemy.

Captain Wastin and I had to wait until our road was mineswept before we could start our jeep trip over a potholed lane that would have delighted a chiropractor.

"At night," the captain told me, "Viet-Minh peasants dig holes in the roadbed and fill them with soft earth. A jeep, hitting one of the soft spots at 40 miles per hour, ends up in the ditch."

I remembered that Howard Brody, *Collier's* artist, had been hospitalized with a back injury after a jeep trip over French Indo-China roads.

The mines were an equal menace. Despite daily mine-sweeping, jeeps and trucks came to grief as twisted and burned-out wrecks in the roadside ditches attested.

I saw food baskets bounce off the tops of disintegrating Asiatic buses, packed to capacity, as they bounced over the holes in the road.

Viet-Namese and Moung coolie women worked at repairing the roads.

"Our human bulldozers," Wastin called them.

We saw other female "bulldozers" filling in paddies along the "Little Maginot Line." This was to raise the field of view from pillbox apertures and prevent guerrillas from creeping close with bazookas, Wastin told me.

In front of one pillbox, women were cutting down tough elephant grass to golf-course height so that no enemy could hide in it. Senegalese lookouts sat on platforms in tree crotches high above the ground.

I climbed up to the platform of one of these lookouts. I startled Private Mpogasylvani of Lake Chad but his self-scarred ebony visage frightened me even more.

He was shy, almost demure, as I sketched him. He, like his countrymen, seemed lost in this far-off country. The Senegalese have little money. White soldiers can find companions—camp followers are imported from Fez and Casablanca for the Moroccans. However, the Senegalese have little but each other and the dogs they adopt.

My trip to Luc-Nam, twenty-five miles over rutted roads on the outer defense perimeter, took most of a day and gave me a chance to see some of the Red River delta. Fields were filled with men and women transplanting rice or fishing for carp from basket canoes. Most paddies serve as carp ponds. Scarecrows in coolie hats protect the fish from hawks. There were small boys riding caribou and nude boy and girl bathers. We saw the buttocks and bare breasts of half-submerged maidens.

We stopped at a Buddhist temple. Terra-cotta dragons writhed along its eaves. Inside, an old priest used a Zippo lighter to light the cigarette he was smoking and the shrine candles on the same flame. Outside the temple were the spotted dogs of the countryside that resembled miniature hyenas. Wastin told me that they were a Viet-Namese delicacy and were beaten to death to tenderize their meat.

The road we followed was the famous Mandarin route that stretched from Nanning to Saigon. It paralleled the railroad. The railway was useless now. The Viet-Minh had carried away its rails and ties and gouged out crosswise trenches in the embankment every ten feet.

"You've heard of the 'piano key' sabotage?" Wastin said. "This is a beautiful example of it. Repair is hopeless."

We passed partisan patrols, little men carrying guns and, sometimes, their wives carrying rifles and birdcages. I saw a file of them bringing in prisoners under guard.

The country was changing as we reached the foothills at the delta's edge. I looked in amazement at cities that had been completely leveled by the Viet-Minh. A few heaps of scorched bricks were all that was left of Bac Ninh. A few miles beyond, in the important junction of Phu Lang Thuong, I saw the burnt-out shell of its cathedral—the last building remaining erect in the city. The bridge, blasted by American bombs in World War II, still lay twisted across the river like a prehistoric monster.

After Phu Lang Thuong (the way Wastin pronounced it, it sounded like something Dorothy Lamour would wear), the country became more mountainous. Spanish mules from the Pyrenees carried military packs along the trails. They looked right in that setting.

Suddenly we struck a series of Beau Geste forts. There was one on each hilltop. It was nearly night as we approached Luc Nam. I could hear bugles clarioning from peak to peak. As I watched, tricolors climbed down masts.

Wastin and I had walked into a party. The commandant, scholarly, bespectacled Captain Charles Deschenes of the Vosges, told us the officers of the fort were giving a farewell dinner to young Lieutenant Henri de Galard of Versailles who was going home to Paris for six-months' leave after 30 long months of duty.

We were hailed gladly by young crew-cutted officers. They toasted Lieutenant de Galard with foaming "Moet & Chandon" champagne and kidded him about the girls he would probably conquer back home.

The officers' mess was a bit of France. Its walls were decorated with *Air France* posters and amateur paintings of the Eiffel Tower and Sacré-Coeur. The only pin-up was a framed photograph of an unappetizing 300-pound Montmartre tart, leaning against a lamppost. No doubt the psychology behind the picture was to keep down the battalion's temperature. Someone had ingeniously improvised lamp shades from coolie hats. A gasoline refrigerator was filled with Perrier and Vichy water. Stacks of year-old French and American magazines weighed down an old sofa with springs beginning to spiral through its red plush covering. (This sofa was to be my bed for the night.)

The battalion's doctor, who looked like a younger edition of Groucho Marx with his shoe-brush mustache, shellrim glasses and tilted cigar, turned the conversation to American films.

"How old is the lovely Paulette Goddard?" he asked me. "Is Esther Williams married? I'd be glad to fill the bill if the job is open!"

Despite his French accent, he looked so much like Groucho when he made this last leering comment that I laughed.

He and Wastin plied me with questions about other film actresses until I had to confess the only movie stars I had ever met were male.

Talk switched to the war in the north. The young French officers envied their comrades' cool-weather fighting in "Korée"—I shuddered at this—and were downright jealous when I told of seeing French officers in Geisha houses. Their lips parted when I described men and girls bathing together. This set off a stream of fleshpot reminiscences of Saigon and Hanoi, led by the doctor, who had a fine appreciation of womanhood.

Captain Deschenes broke open a bottle of kirschwasser which his mother had sent him, for a nightcap. It was difficult to drink because the flies that had furnished a background hum as they wheeled over the table during the evening were now attracted by the sweet brandy and stuck to the rims of glasses.

One of the lieutenants began to play records by French *chanteuses* on the record player. The officers were especially proud of Laura Diana's recording of the song of the French Colonial Marines, their corps anthem. It was played and re-played to shouts and uplifted glasses. We heard Piaf and Sablon, too.

At midnight they put me to bed on the red plush couch. I was blissfully unaware of jagged springs. They draped a mosquito net over me, placed a bottle of wine on the floor next to me (in case I got thirsty during the night) and stood about the couch giving a lilting rendition of *Lili Marlene*. I fell asleep under the puffy eyes of the Montmartre tart.

Five-thirty reveille bounced me off the couch in time to join a patrol going on reconnaissance in the "death zone," a five-mile strip between Luc Nam and the Viet-Minh. The doctor presented me with a *chapeau de brousse*.

"You can consider yourself a French Colonial Marine from now on," he said.

The patrol's objective was the searching of a group of farm hamlets several miles deep in the zone, suspected of harboring guerrillas. The first mile was comparatively pleasant. The sun was still low in the sky. When we left the dikes, however, and cut across rice country toward the farms, the going got rough. I lost one of my moccasins to the glue-like mud that sucked up above my ankles. It didn't make very much difference because, by this time, I was wet to the waist and my remaining shoe squished water whenever we crossed a dry path.

Going through a swamp, I stepped on something alive and round that slithered under my bare foot. The doctor had told me to watch out for pythons. I plunged frantically ahead without looking down and finally caught up with the patrol—that had long since outdistanced me—under the impetus of fear.

I proved a new taste treat for clouds of insects. Cardinal-color dragonflies dive-bombed at me, mosquitoes stabbed my arms and legs, clammy gnats stuck to my eyelids and blood-bloated leeches hung from my calves. I agreed with Captain Wastin: "Every time you squash one, you squash your own blood."

The squad deployed about the farmhouses and closed in slowly. The farmers had seen us coming and waited for us in the courtyard. The Viet-Namese searched the houses and found no one in them. Three young men were seized from the courtyard group and marched protestingly away for questioning at the fort.

Lunch was an event, as always in a French post, no matter how small. There was always a printed menu. Today's included:

—;— MENU DÉJEUNER —;—

HORS D'OEUVRES VARIÉS

POISSON MAYONNAISE

PETITS ROULEAUX LOCAUX

COTELETTES DE PORC

PURÉE de P. de T.

BEIGNETS BANANES

CAFÉ

TRAMINER — BEAUJOLAIS

Et au Nom de Dieu . . .

— VIVE LA COLONIALE —

VIVE L'AMÉRICAIN

I was introduced to Armand, the wine-drinking parrot of the fort, who swigged Burgundy. His sergeant owner, practicing an economy, tried to fool Armand with French GI powdered wine and water but the parrot vindictively spilled it as fast as it was poured into his cup.

I was conducted around the fort and to neighboring forts to see the defenses. Every known type of defensive device was used. Stockades of logs, for example, were lashed to the mud and brick towers to absorb the shock of enemy bazookas. For my benefit, several rounds of mortar fire was directed on a suspected village in the rice plains below.

Dinner that night was intended as a special treat for me. We moved from the officers' mess to the Chinese-operated canteen in the refugees' "shantytown" which surrounded the walls of the fort.

The canteen's Chinese proprietress welcomed us with a glittering mouthful of gold teeth. Her charms, apparent through her shiny black coolie pajamas, were an old story to the officers who greeted her with the familiarity of a "daughter of the regiment."

We ate by lantern light. It was difficult to identify the dishes we were served. I was all too aware, however, of chicken claws groping to the surface in a thick soup. The stringy tentacles that trailed over the edge of another dish were identified for me as the river octopi Viet-Namese love.

The chopsticks were well suited to military shop talk of maneuver and encirclement. They were used, too, to describe the bosom-heavy contours of the officers' favorite actresses. They were not so handy, however, for picking up the slippery cherries we were served for dessert.

Unexpected entertainment coincided with the serving of the after-dinner wines. A huge brown rat cavorted like a crazy ballerina on the rafter directly over the dinner table. Wastin kept his flashlight spotted on him. The young officers laid small bets as to whether he would stay aloft or take a suicidal plunge to the table. The rat stayed aloft.

I had found the doctor most amusing and was delighted when he hitched a ride to Hanoi with us. He claimed that all our talk of girls had made a trip to the local fleshpots a pure physical necessity. He blamed most of this on me.

182

"It was those stories about the Geishas. Think I can get one of the Hanoi girls to take a bath with me? I'm sure they're afraid of soap and water, though," he remarked disconsolately.

We left him on a corner of a Hanoi main street. At last sight, he was pushing open the door of the Paramount, local jitterbug palace. He looked back at us with a typical Groucho leer and raised his cigar in a final salute.

I flew in a Junker to Laichau in the mountains on the Burmese border. The plane carried blankets for the garrison there. As we passed other isolated outposts en route, we dropped by parachute such unusual items as champagne for officers and live, kicking goats for Moroccans.

The lumbering ship scraped through narrow mountain passes on its way to the cut-off garrison. Below us, as we flew over enemy territory, I could see distinctly a human pack train carrying Viet-Minh supplies. From 150,000 to 200,000 coolies trudge over rainswept mountain trails and blasted highways, carrying guns, ammunition, food and medicine, sometimes even artillery dismantled and carried piece by piece from Red China to the enemy. This coolie transport system is the only way that Viet-Minh can supply their armies.

We made a pancake landing in a very small valley beneath the fort. The plane was quickly unloaded. I had time enough for a glimpse of the region's famous Thai beauties, elegant and stately in white blouses, long clinging skirts and flat coolie hats. They walked like queens, taking no notice of either gaping correspondents or Moroccan guards. I did not dare miss the plane's return trip to Hanoi for I might be stuck for days here, in the event of bad weather striking.

On the return trip, betel-nut-chewing wives of Viet-Namese businessmen prayed in fright and were sick in paper bags. They had started being sick even before the propeller was turned.

Two weeks after my trip to Luc Nam, the Viet-Minh launched the first full-scale attack of a new war season on that fort.

I flew in a fragile Storch-Fiesler to Mon Cay on the Chinese border. I had the sensation I was riding on a bird's back. We flew over the rail line that connects Hanoi with the port of Haiphong on the Gulf of Tonkin. Beneath us stretched the entire delta, a sea of rice fields crisscrossed with canals and hair-thin roads.

As we neared the port city, we passed over wrecked freight and passenger cars. The line had been dynamited by saboteurs just that morning. Derricks were attempting to lift the prone engine to the tracks.

We turned north at Haiphong to follow the coast over the unreal rock-strewn Baie d-Along. Thousands of monolithic hundred-foot-high rock towers reared in fanciful forms. Wind and tide had carved these rocks into surrealistic shapes. I could see the brown sails of fishing junks under their arches and grottos.

For centuries, my pilot told me, this treacherous coast had been the haunt of Chinese pirates. The bay is a maze of reefs and shoals. The sheer cliffs are often shrouded in ghostly fog. It is a mariner's nightmare. Today, junks carrying rice, salt, guns, bales of counterfeit currency, to the Viet-Minh play hide and seek with French navy craft. During the day, junks and sampans hide in creeks waiting for dusk. If French patrol ships are in the waters outside, the boats are beached and they wait in jungle cover.

About halfway up the coast, we flew over open amphitheaters of black coal. I could see coolies working the thick surface veins. The French are anxious to hold on to these rich coal deposits.

When I entered the barracks of the Foreign Legionnaires at Mon Cay, the bearded mercenaries greeted me in a half-dozen languages.

They were hardly the tough rogues of legend. They were modest men, most of them, and they were in Indo-China for adventure, not to escape some dark past of robbery or murder.

Sergeant Carlos Inverizzi of Naples was my escort, a glistening-eyed man with a Mephisto-phelian beard. He introduced me to a cross-section of the corps. Sergeant Siegfried Hoffman of Wilhelmshafen was a veteran of Rommel's *Afrika Korps*. Fighting was not new to him. The blond Hoffman was typical of the Germans who make up 30 per cent of the Legion. Private Georges Galichnik of the Russian Crimea and Polish Private Henry Olesinski were two of the many Legion-naires who come from the Iron Curtain countries. Galichnik and I eagerly exchanged notes on the Crimea (I had been there in 1934). Galichnik had been captured by the Germans near Moscow and liked them. After the war his friend, Heinz Hess, had joined the Legion. To be with him "and to fight Communism," Galichnik had joined up.

Olesinski was a Communist-hater of the first order. He even hated the color red.

Private Jose Diego of Pamplona, Spain, had fought Franco in the Spanish Civil War. As an anarchist, he told me, he was not welcome anywhere "except here in the Legion."

I had the usual champagne lunch with Captain Marcel Le Testu of Rouen. The small, intel-lectual-looking captain wore the Abraham Lincoln-type beard affected by Left Bank students. He talked intelligently about the paintings that decorated the mess. Here, in this furthermost outpost of Indo-China, were good color prints including a Van Gogh self-portrait, a Renoir nude and a Cézanne apple arrangement.

184

The captain thought I might like to visit the local Chinese pottery plant. Le Testu introduced me to the foreman as an artist. Immediately I was handed a brush and palette and seated in front of a row of unglazed clay bowls.

While the Chinese artists of the pottery and the Legionnaires formed a gallery about me, I painted—rather crudely, I fear—a set of bowls and a water jug with figures of French soldiers and sailors from Louis XIV to World War II. I presented them to the captain as a gift for the mess.

I gazed into almond-shaped eyes—Communist eyes—through field glasses as I stood atop a pillbox on the river's edge. The eyes belonged to a Chinese Communist soldier who was scanning us through glasses from the other side of the river. Captain Le Testu asked me not to sketch or take photos as I might draw rifle fire. Snapshots had been answered with rifle fire in the past.

I had a closer look at the Communists when I marched or jeeped with Legionnaires to frontier outposts.

My trip to Saigon was cut short by an upcoming operation in the delta which I was eager to cover.

I was in the southern city long enough, however, to feel out its grim spirit of fear and foreboding.

Outwardly, this metropolis went about its business and pleasure as usual. Its 20,000 French rode on the wide boulevards in smart cars and motorized pedi-cabs or shopped in stores filled with merchandise from the Rue de la Paix, the Rue St.-Honoré and Boulevard St.-Germain. They strolled in the Jardin Botanique with their wives and sweethearts and fed French bread to the elephants. Officers played tennis and swam at the Club Sportif and watched shapely French girls, spilling out of Bikini bathing suits that split them up the back, sport in the pool.

At the Venise and the Grande Monde cafés, soldiers and sailors drank and danced or experimented with Chinese girls in the nearby Chinese city of Cholon.

The harbor was jammed with the traffic of war, cruisers, private ships and junks. The atmosphere was heavy: there was no breeze stirring. The flags on the ships hung limp except for the tricolor on a river craft's mast that flew proudly. When I came close, I saw that it was made of iron.

Underneath the surface gaiety, however, ran an ominous tone. There was fear in Saigon. The Viet-Minh, though not in great army strength in the south, operates close to the city. The enemy advertises its presence in a number of sinister ways.

At night I could hear the coughing of mortars across the river. A cautious American ECA administrator, whom I visited, has his home guarded by rifle-carrying private policemen on 24-hour guard duty. The wife of a correspondent refused to leave her apartment at any time. We had cocktails in a sidewalk café and found, to our horror, that it was bombed a few hours after we left it. Another café, crowded with dancers, was wrecked by a pencil grenade thrown by a passing cyclist, during my stay. Many people were killed or maimed.

I was glad to return to the comparative safety of Hanoi, even though it was in the center of the war.

I dined with Major General Francois Gonzales de Linares in his rambling mansion near the cathedral. On first sight, I realized how apt was the nickname *"La Cigogne"* ("The Stork") given him by his men. He was extraordinarily tall with a deep-chested, heavy body supported by needle-thin, knock-kneed legs. He had shed his uniform for dinner and was wearing comfortable white sports clothes and white shoes. The towering three-star general was commandant of the French forces of Northern Viet-Nam.

Again, there was the printed menu, the champagne and wines, and after-dinner cheese. White-robed, black-turbaned Viet-Namese servants glided smoothly about the 30-foot-long table under the direction of a Moroccan major-domo who was splendid in a black and gold striped turban. General Linares was courtly and affable: his entourage of young aides, led by his monocled Chef de Cabinet emulated his gallant manner.

Over Scotch and ginger ale in the drawing room, I talked alone with the sixty-one-year-old General.

"You have been to Mon Cay," the General said. "You know there are 250,000 well-equipped Chinese troops between that border city and Nanning—and nothing to prevent their making an attack at any time but a string of isolated outposts that could put up only a holding action. If they should attack, they could overwhelm us by superior numbers and with their heavy equipment, pierce our defenses. We would surely lose all of north Indo-China, unless we had immediate and strong help from your country. We would need American troops as well as planes and tanks."

He sighed deeply.

"As it stands now, it is a war of stalemate. While the Viet-Minh outnumber us, they cannot pass our defense lines. Our fortifications are too strong. They would need heavy artillery and armor to break our lines. We only hold about one-sixth of the country—and it's useless for us to think of conquering the other five-sixths. This is the toughest kind of terrain—paddy, mountain and jungle country. Furthermore, there is no such thing as an old-fashioned battle here. It's guerrilla warfare. If I were to send out a strong force, provided I had it, into enemy territory, they would be ambushed and cut off."

He described the present pattern of combat in Indo-China, such as it was.

"Generally speaking, there are four kinds of villages on and within the perimeter: reliable villages which we arm and trust fully; friendly villages which we do not arm; villages that are half friendly and half hostile; and definitely unfriendly villages into which the enemy usually infiltrates. The action you will see tomorrow will be against this last kind of village." He leaned forward, his long legs outstretched so that he looked more stork-like than ever. "What happens when we 'take' a village like this? To be honest, we only make more enemies—send more civilians over to the Viet-Minh side, psychologically at least! The enemy escapes by underground passage to the next town. Innocent people are hurt and killed, the village is destroyed by artillery and napalm—and the civilians hate us more than ever. You will see all this tomorrow for yourself."

It sounded like a hopeless method of conquest.

"We have an ace up our sleeve, as you Americans would say," the General continued. "We are now rushing the training of Viet-Namese troops. We will send them into these infiltrated areas to garrison villages eventually. When the civilians see it is their own people and not the 'foreigner' who is coming, they will be cooperative. It is our great hope to set up a chain of village garrisons throughout the whole of the country within the perimeter. This, of course, is if the Chinese do not attack."

I remarked that the paddy war must be a severe drain on France.

"It has been, on our officer man power especially. Young French captains are graduating from St.-Cyr to come directly out here and die. We are killing off the cream of our military youth—it is a situation very much like that in England in the beginning of World War II, when the 'first sons' of Britain were killed off in the RAF at such a terrific rate."

"How are the Viet-Namese as soldiers?" I asked.

"They are excellent soldiers. I have seldom seen training so well repaid. But we must equip them completely. That is another reason we need so much aid from America. We used to fly over Viet-Minh territory without a second thought. Now we are greeted by antiaircraft fire—the Chinese Communists' present to the Viet-Minh. I lost sleep for an entire week after I discovered the Viet-Minh had new weapons."

186

He questioned me now about the Korean war. He was intensely interested in my thoughts on the outcome of that action.

"When the Chinese are no longer concentrating on Korea, they may turn their attention to us," the General worried. "We live in dread of that time. If we fail in Indo-China, the Communists will have a springboard from which to drive west into Thailand and Burma, south to Singapore, possibly even east to Mayala. If we lose Indo-China, the democratic world loses all of Southeast Asia."

We sat in silence for a moment. Then, in a lighter tone, the General said, "But you must see my garden before you leave. It is my great diversion from the war and I am very proud of it."

We rose. He leaned down to look at the sketches I had been making of him while he talked. Frowning slightly, he pointed to one of the drawings.

"Mr. Groth, you have been more generous to me than nature! I do have a large nose—my Spanish ancestors gave it to me—but you have exaggerated it."

I altered the sketch and he led me happily into the garden. He called for a flashlight. The light flickered over heavy beards of moss dripping from the banyan trees. He showed me his enormous peonies with great pride.

He rode back to the press hostel with me in his black Hotchkiss. On the way he outlined the operation of the next day.

The French objective was aimed at eliminating an estimated three battalions of Viet-Minh guerrillas operating in a 50-mile-square area 35 miles southeast of Hanoi. The plan was to encircle the area and close in to the center, cleaning out suspected villages one by one. On our way to the hostel, troop-carrying trucks rumbled past us on their way to the Red River. For two days, landing craft had been assembling in unusual numbers along the river front. I wondered if the attack would really be a surprise to the Viet-Minh.

The General waited while I put on my khakis and hurriedly gathered my gear. We drove to the river. It was pitch black. An officer waited with a flashlight to conduct me to my boat. I said goodnight to the General and he wished me *"Bonne chance"* before he drove off.

17 • Operation Mop-Up

I was guided aboard an LCI (Landing Craft Infantry) by the beam of the officer's flashlight. Muffled orders and grunting Diesels signaled the beginning of our journey. We were joining other units on the Canal des Bambous for a dawn attack.

It was quiet aboard. Viet-Namese paratroopers smoked tensely, cigarette tips glowing through their cupped fingers. There was no sound as we swished forward through the dark other than the pulsing of motors and the rhythmic chirping of frogs. A night bird cried angrily as we passed. Aquatic birds, disturbed by our passage, fluttered bankward with a quick flapping of wings.

At midnight the moon popped suddenly over the low landscape's rim, silvering the river and ships. There was a delay of an hour when one of the barges ran onto a sandbar. The column of iron barges nosed left and right as they wove around the bends of the winding river.

As we turned into the Canal des Bambous, light began to grow in the East. Against the carmine sky, I could see the silhouetted shapes of men and women carrying baskets to early market.

At a megaphone command, the column of barges—orange colored in the dawn light—wheeled toward the canal's left bank. Ramps were dropped. Torrents of paratroopers poured ashore, deploying along the bank. The far bank of the canal was fringed with Moroccan troops, impatiently waiting for the barges to ferry them into a position on the right flank of the Viet-Namese. I crossed over to join them, and then re-crossed with them.

I took my position with the fierce hawk-nosed men in bush hats along the lee side of the bank and waited for H hour. I knew that when the action started, I would have little chance to make sketches or get names. So I smoked and talked pidgin French with Mimouhli Afrain of Mouzert, twenty-seven-year-old private second class, and Haddou ou Haddou of Fez, forty-year-old private first class. Haddou traded his hat badge for my Zippo lighter. The two spoke a few words of English they had picked up from American GI's in the last war. They would say "Lucky Strike" and point to their mouths.

To my left, a group of French officers with mustaches and beards argued over maps, using their canes to point out landscape details. Several, stripped to the waist, carried umbrellas. I made a quick sketch of Captain Jean Felix Gabrielli of Corsica, the most picturesque of the group. He was pleased when I told him he looked like a character from *La Bohème* with his Louis Napoleon III mustache and goatee, big pants and map case that resembled an artist's portfolio. The basketball shoes he wore gave an incongruous note to his artist's costume.

Our immediate objective was the village of Hao Khe, about a mile away. We spotted it by a defense tower that rose above the trees and bamboo' growing out of the paddies and swamps. The landscape was motionless except for fishermen paddling in a basket canoe across a blue-green lake and a boy riding the hump of a water buffalo silhouetted minutely against a distant silver stretch of water.

Immediately below us an old woman sat in the doorway of a hut, pulling impatiently at quickening intervals at a rice-straw rope attached to a huge net suspended from bamboo poles. A white rag was wrapped around her head. She was fishing for silver fish like the tiny ones drying on the branches of a tree between us and the hut.

Haddou drew my attention with hisses of appreciation to a young woman washing clothes in a paddy. Her buttocks were clearly defined through the worn material of her skirt.

Suddenly, the peace of the rustic landscape was shattered by the croupy coughing of distant mortars. Shells began to splatter in paddies along the horizon. The civilians disappeared except for the old woman fishing below us. A flight of egrets sprang skyward from swamp water.

Then the attack began.

A squad filtered into a tunnel of bamboo and emerged waist-deep in a paddy, the men holding their rifles high above their heads. Another squad fanned out to take a cluster of three huts 100 yards ahead. Through binoculars, I saw three men race across a farmyard while the others covered. As they poked their rifles into doors and windows, a woman and three children ran out in the courtyard. From the house, there was a short burst of tommy-gun fire, and a man was dragged to where the woman and children stood.

A Moroccan pulled the wounded man to his feet and pushed him through the rice to the canal embankment, the blood spurting from his shoulder and pinking the water in his wake.

I ran down the path to get a sketch of the prisoner. As I passed the old woman, I noticed that her eyes were blind with trachoma. Behind her were several children, their eyes watching over her shoulder. The sketch done, I rejoined Haddou.

Other squads skirmished through farmhouses in their path while spotter planes spiraled slowly over the larger villages. As the scattered fire became more insistent, we plunged along a deep ditch in the direction of Hao Khe. A frightened water buffalo broke the water before us in plunges. Birds sprayed from the trees. Frogs plopped into the water with every step.

Small-arms fire chattered around us. A bearded soldier wounded in the upper thigh bloodied his carrier as he was brought past us. The wounded Moroc was alternately groaning and grinning, depending on whom he passed—groans for the officers, grins for his fellow infantrymen. The Viet-Namese soldier carrying him just groaned.

The terrain in the delta is as much an enemy as the Viet-Minh. Swamp and paddies surround islet-like villages. From the Canal des Bambous stretched a mile of the meanest fighting country I had ever seen. The soldiers and their human pack train—coolies carrying haversacks, ammo and Alsatian beer—were in and out of the water every few minutes, sometimes plunging shoulder high and keeping their weapons dry with difficulty. Near me, a cursing Moroccan pulled a snake from around his ankle and smashed its head against a log.

Solid ground was rare. An occasional fallen tree provided a bridge—and sped up the advance. Riflemen poured across the slippery trunks of fallen trees.

As we neared the village, the Moroccans dug in along a ravine, and fired into the houses among the thick clumps of bamboos. The officers were profiled against the sky. When I asked one of them why he stood when he commanded his men to lie flat, he replied, "As an example to

our soldiers," adding with a wry laugh, "of our bravery."

I understood why Linares had said the French officer class was being depleted!

Our shells now hammered away at Hao Khe. Suddenly, the high tower crumbled and disappeared. A moment later, a piece of red earth as big as a bank building was hurtled into the sky.

Shells falling short geysered the surfaces of paddies and fragments fell close to the skirmishers out front. They ran quickly back to the protection of our ravine. Dead carp floated on the surface of ponds. A kingfisher whirring through a ditch struck my bush hat. Thousands of butterflies, their wings embroidered with green, and as large as gloves, suddenly drifted by at eye level, obscuring our vision.

With a silence as loud as the shelling itself, the bombardment ceased. The sound of firing beyond the village told us that other elements of our attacking force were closing in. We splashed through overflowing paddies, past brightly colored shrines, into the outskirts of the smoking village. At its ruined gates, a group of four black-clad men, a village elder and three boys, waited. The old man held a bamboo pole from which hung a white rag of surrender. The Moroccans ran past them into the village without a glance. As I passed them, I was reminded of Rodin's sculpture group, *The Burghers of Calais*. A French officer accepted their surrender.

Every now and then, we heard a burst of machine-gun fire being poured into the holes and tunnels where the enemy might be hidden. I remembered what Linares had said about the Viet-Minh escaping from one village to the next through these tunnels.

In the brush and hedges surrounding the village, women and naked children crouched in fear. The recent shelling had sent them scurrying into the thin safety of foliage. They did not look up as we passed. I offered a piece of chocolate from my musette bag to a child who looked up. His mother snatched it from his hand and flung it at my feet. I was a death-carrying stranger, like the others—to her.

Rooted-out tree trunks pointed accusingly; a headless pig sprawled across our path, his legs in the air. Pig-hating Mohammedan Moroccans plunged knee-deep into a ditch to avoid it.

I looked into a hut. The door had been enlarged by a shell burst. I could see the debris of a room, bits of pots, joss sticks, and a metal crucifix. The combination of Buddhist and Christian talismans had not protected this home.

Two hyena-like dogs, minus tails, snapped at bare Moroccan ankles. They were methodically kicked into silence.

The village had been secured. The soldiers now spread out in every direction, looking for items to liberate. They didn't find much—a little food and an occasional jar of rice wine. In the heat of the sun, they broke out their rations—bottles of warm beer, tins of cheese, huge loaves of bread, and wine powder to be poured into their canteens. The powder did little more than kill the taste of the water, but that was a blessing. Moroccans held live chickens by the legs over the floors of burning buildings, searing their feathers off.

I shared the bread and beer but passed up the chicken.

After eating, they stripped down and sat in pools to wash off the sweat of their morning's work. The Mohammedans would count the dip toward the five daily ablutions they must make— one before each of their five daily prayers.

In the action around Hao Khe, I had seen a graphic illustration of the pattern of fighting General Linares had described to me. There was no need to go further. Any other action in this operation would be a repetition of Hao Khe.

I added up the morning's achievements: a village burned, buildings destroyed, animals dead, children branded with fear. Soon the Viet-Minh would move back and take reprisals on the villagers because the Viet-Namese and French had been here.

It seemed like a hopeless war. I was glad that the action along the Canal des Bambous had been my last reportorial assignment in Asia.

18 · The Rest of Asia

The rest of Asia flashed past my eyes as quickly as a stack of picture postcards flipped by a nervous thumb.

I felt a compulsion to see India, Kashmir, Thailand, Afghanistan, Pakistan, and Turkey *now,* while there was still a chance for me to do. Some of them were on my route back to New York. Most of them bordered the Communist states of Russia and China. The way things had been going, they might be sealed off to me before I could make a second visit.

Though I was free now to enjoy these countries as a sightseer, I found myself making sketches and notes just as I had while I was still on a formal assignment. My impressions follow.

Thailand

Bangkok was choked with golden temples and palaces, as advertised. It was off season for temple dancers though $50 bought me a private performance.

I found the city a bustling boomtown. The intellectuals worried about an eventual Communist attack, but it was at once apparent to me—as to every other traveler—that the country has already been invaded and at least partially conquered by the Western salesmen who pour in on every plane.

Americans honked angry auto horns along muddy, potholed streets, sending sun-drugged Thailanders sprinting. The horns drowning the soft tinkling of temple bells, symbolized the new economic order that has come to the "never-never land" of *Anna and the King of Siam.*

Even more symbolic were the black dentures and bridges I saw in a modern dentist's shop. They were a concession to the betel-nut-chewing populace.

196

The average Thailander who has always led a lazy, Garden-of-Eden existence, oblivious to who ruled him so long as he was able to pluck his supper from the tree in whose shade he lay, has been affected by the changes from the West. He has acquired a taste for Philip Morris cigarettes. He sports a Ronson lighter—if he can afford it. He is on speaking terms with the Ford '51. He likes Betty Grable and Danny Kaye movies.

The upper classes have been completely conquered. I window-shopped in ugly, hastily built structures of plank and brick, whose shelves and display tables bulged with Western goods. I saw strange shop fellows: a Corona typewriter in the midst of a display of Clapp's Baby Food; a stack of Goodyear tires leaning incongruously against a counter piled with Maidenform bras and Munsingwear nylons. In the midst of this chaos of tires, nylons, and typewriters, rich Thailanders and their wives wandered distractedly, happy as children in a candy shop. They were buying gleaming Frigidaires, deep-freezes, auto jacks, camera lenses, Aerosol bombs, and athletic supporters with a delirious disregard of price tags.

Despite the dragging fear many Thailanders have of Communist invasion, Bangkok had a nonchalant attitude toward the future. I would have supposed that a small country surrounded by disturbed and threatened neighbors would be preparing itself for eventual attack. But I found that in Thailand, in place of Universal Military Training, every youth serves a period of training as a novitiate Buddhist priest. The young monks, with their cropped heads, effeminate faces and saffron robes, were everywhere in the city. Their begging bowls were always filled: they rode streetcars free. This was obviously the happiest time of their lives.

My time in Thailand was short. I could hardly see the natives for the Americans in the city. Christian missionaries and Fulbright exchange professors and their wives (from Midwestern denominational colleges)—prototypes of Grant Wood's grim-visaged "American Gothics"—turned their faces and lifted their skirts to avoid fellow Americans, branch managers and sales representatives who drank whiskey and briskly chased Thailand beauties.

There was a small, more constructive element in Thailand—earnest teams of ECA men who drained swamps, fought malaria and carried on rural health programs. Information libraries, military commissions and *The Voice of America* were here with the purpose of making good allies of the Thailanders. But as I looked at the languorous barefooted men lolling on their food-laden porches, watching teak-log rafts drift by in the river, or at the ill-equipped army and the toy navy with its rusting boats, I doubted that the backs of these lotus-eaters could ever be stiffened sufficiently to resist Communist aggression.

I was to remember Bangkok in terms of the view from my hotel lawn—the view that had so frustrated me on my first evening, when I wanted to steep myself in the romance of Siam as I had imagined it. Somehow it epitomized the exotic country's surrender to Western commerce—the huge Caltex sign that blocked the view of graceful temple spires and jewel-encrusted palaces on the other side of the river.

India

I saw India's millions through a haze of dust and dancing heat—two hundred thousand festival-crazed Hindus celebrating their Dusserah holiday on a sun-scorched plain between Old and New Delhi. Whole villages of peasant women jangled as they clustered under a gnome-like statue of their beloved saint, Gandhi. Their ankles bore layer upon layer of bangles. Some feminine arms were covered with entire sleeves of silver. These walking silvermines wore the family wealth—what there was of it.

My artist's eye was delighted by a field of moving flowers—women in vari-colored saris of pink, gold and blue. The colors were unbelievably intense in the hundred-degree heat of the plain. They strolled with their husbands, who wore the white boat-shaped caps of the Congress Party and kept their shirts outside their trousers.

Pinkish sweet-eyed oxen exercised their holy prerogative as they shouldered their large bodies through the crowd. They were followed by ragged half-naked "untouchables" (straight out of *Mother India*), women and children who eagerly scooped the smoking dung into fuel baskets.

It was on this plain that I first saw those figures who disturbed me most of all I saw in India. They still haunt my thoughts. These were wild-haired Sadhus or holy men who competed with one another for attention in the most horrifying ways imaginable.

Their completely naked bodies were painted with blue ashes and mud. One wore his tongue hanging bloodily to his chest. It was pierced by a spike. Another had buttons sewn on his cheeks. Others, in continuous war with feeble constitutions, whipped their limbs with chains and slashed themselves with knives. Later, I was to see other holy horror men hanging by their feet from crosses, sleeping on beds of nails, and entombed alive. I peered into a mountain cave inhabited by a holy man who never appeared except to take offerings of food left on the cave's lip. He had been the neophyte of a former occupant and had moved in to spend his life beside the skeleton of the ex-tenant.

The Sadhus had competition—dozens of beggars who scraped their disease-swollen limbs over the yellow dust-covered ground. They dragged at saris and legs.

I had my first, fleeting glimpse of Pandit Nehru that day. His arrival, late in the afternoon, caused a near-stampede. Policemen and soldiers worked heroically to keep the crowd from trampling their hero.

My first impressions of the country were of masses of people—unforgettable odors (the smell of India was never to leave my clothes even after I had left the land)—and a vivid variety of costumes that were almost overpowering to my artist's sensibilities.

On my way to Agra, I saw much of India's central plain from the train window.

I had always heard how the Hindu religion interfered with the Indian's struggle for existence. Here I saw vividly the tragic consequences of their unquestioning adherence to religious taboos.

Troops of sacred monkeys gamboled and grimaced at emaciated farmers who watched them eating their precious crops. Darkening swarms of locusts aided their ringtailed allies in eating the cupboard bare until there was little left for the farmers' starving children and scarecrow cows.

I saw more of these starving farmers and their families on an auto trip to ancient Fatehpur Sikri. They hungered along the road while herds of spotted deer and other game grazed fearlessly near them. Hinduism prevents hunting, too.

I learned that a dead animal is fair game. On our way to the old city, we passed the sprawled prehistoric-looking shape of a camel that had dropped dead a few minutes before. Vultures pecked at its eyes. An hour later, when we passed again, its precious skin and meat had been ripped away by peasants. All that seemed left of the carcass that was now covered by vultures was its gleaming white skeleton.

There is not enough food for India's people and their domesticated animals. There is no fodder for the cows and consequently they give little milk. Starving shadowy dogs roam the streets, searching for scraps. I saw them fighting with vultures for bits of offal. At the Delhi Burning Ghats, they impatiently dug their faces into the hot ashes of freshly cremated bodies as they tried to pull out bones. Their noses burnt, they howled and yelled.

I had been under the mistaken impression that India was a country of "passive resistance." But everywhere I saw military activity. Billboards at crossroads called for army and navy volunteers to defend India. Smart turbaned infantrymen swung along roads. Barracks at New Delhi were filled with trainees. Military planes buzzed overhead.

198

Village maidens - Delhi

An Indian officer engineer whom I met later in Kashmir was frank in his criticism of his country's military investment. He felt that the "guns instead of butter" policies of the Congress Party were diverting money needed for the feeding of the Indian people.

"It would be better spent on food, education and health," he said.

I looked forward to seeing the Taj Mahal by full moon. Neither the moon nor the Taj disappointed me, but I had not counted on sharing the spectacle with 5,000 romantic couples. A capacity crowd filled its walks and lawns, "Ooh-ing and "Ah-ing" in forty different languages.

Outside the gate, it was like a giant drive-in movie.

Traffic police directed cars into a huge parking lot. There were soft drink and souvenir stands doing a boom business. Boy Scouts with staves kept visitors on the one-way footpath. I thought, disillusionedly, that the one thing that was missing were spotlights.

Politically, India seemed to me the biggest banana republic in the world. The country seemed to be being ruled by amateurs. After the British left, thousands of inexperienced men of the Congress Party inherited the complicated machinery of government. Men with little know-how headed vast

engineering projects. I met dozens of American industrial trouble shooters who were flown to India by their companies to unknot grave tangles brought about by inefficient native engineers. They told me that young Indians with the engineering background of a new M.I.T. graduate were supervising construction projects costing millions.

Railroad service is rapidly wearing out and not being replaced rapidly enough. The postal service is corrupt. When I gave letters to the desk clerk at my Delhi hotel to be posted, he advised me to register them because, as he said, if I did not the stamps would be stolen from the envelopes in the post office itself. He also advised me to mail packages after I had left the country.

The British are badly missed. Dozens of shopkeepers told me that they wished their old rulers would return. The minorities had been protected by paternal British rule. The untouchable's lot is as hopeless as ever. Though the Congress Party has passed laws "emancipating" him, in practice he is still the untouchable. He and his children empty the chamberpots and sweep the streets of India. By law, his children can now sit in classrooms with the children of higher caste. In actuality, they sit alone, because the parents of the other children remove them. Before the partition, there was escape from their abysmal status by their embracing Mohammedanism or Christianity. Today, the untouchable would be entering an unprotected minority if he did this. The British created opportunities for all minorities. The Hindus take care only of the Hindus.

The military elite displays an open emulation of their former British masters. Young officers wearing English-style uniforms twirl swagger sticks and curl mustaches in almost comic imitation of the departed British officer sahibs.

Bearers who had served the British appeared at every turn to produce tattered letters of recommendation from the sahibs.

To me, it was a realization of Aziz's prophecy to his English friend at the end of Forster's magnificent *A Passage to India:*

"We may hate one another, but we hate you most. We shall get rid of you; yes, we shall drive every blasted Englishman into the sea and then—and then, you and I shall be friends."

India is fertile ground for Communist agitation, as has been proved by the recent election there. Liberty has not been the panacea its leaders hoped it would be. The majority of Indians still live as wretchedly as ever. The restless malcontent that was formerly directed against the British will quite possibly be directed now at the Congress Party.

I could not see that there was much hope of India's becoming a staunch ally of the West in the coming showdown against Communism.

Kashmir

Kashmir, with its fatal, breathtaking natural beauty, is the unfortunate part of an unhappy triangle with India and Pakistan fighting for its favor.

I made my debut in a blanket and astrakhan hat of local vintage. (I had come from 100-degree Indian heat to 30-degree Kashmir cold.) This odd costume did not prevent me from being immediately identified as an American tourist.

Srinagar tonga drivers engaged in a knock-down, drag-'em-out fight over my baggage. (A tonga is a one-horse cart.) They had not seen a tourist for days. The British have gone and tourists are rare. Starving Kashmirites who sell goods and servants hound the infrequent visitor.

I was a target for every local huckster. As I rode the bouncing cart to my hotel, sharp-faced men in pin-striped suits and caracul fezzes cycled alongside, shouting invitations to visit their shops or rent their houseboats. My driver, their sympathetic ally (he was probably a ten-per-center), stopped beating his scarecrow horse, slowing him to a walk, and there was no outdistancing the insistent hawkers.

A horde of them barred the entrance to the hotel. They slipped their business cards and ragged testimonials from past satisfied customers into my pockets as I thrust through them. To get rid of them, I hired the likeliest-looking as guide and bearer. However, as I entered the privacy of my room, he produced a list of shops and of owners of houseboats "available at reduced rates" through his auspices.

The frantic businessmen of Srinagar continually slipped cards under my door and banged on my windows. I tried taking a lone walk along a wooden path. They jumped like Mohawk Indians from behind every tree. Fezzed men with fixed smiles lured me into Cheap John's, Suffering Moses and Subhana The Worst to try to sell me shopworn rugs and shawls, papier-mâché trays and carved cigarette boxes. Outside the shops, beggars, with nothing to sell but their horror of elephantiasis-swollen limbs, barricaded my way and flung back coins they thought too small.

Riding in the gondola-like taxis on the canals and lakes might have been pleasant but shoals of seaborne merchants kept up with us, stroke for stroke, blotting out the beauteous view as they unfurled carpets and shawls. As we passed under canal bridges, they dropped a white snow of business cards on us.

I never visited the Stream of the Rug Sellers, the Canal of the Fur Merchants or the Klong of the Carvers. Instead, *they* visited me. At times, I felt there must be 10,000 sellers versus a dozen buyers.

The life of Srinagar is bound to the fast-flowing Jhelum, fed by Himalayan snows, bordered by rickety wooden houses that never saw paint. The river's floating population lives in Noah's Ark-type wooden boats without windows, but with truck gardens on their roofs. Their bathtub is the river; they drink the river's water, wash their laundry and their donkeys in it, and use it for their two annual baths. They wash dishes, dump garbage and urinate—all in the Jhelum.

The wooden houses are Tudor-like in architecture. Parts of the river have a Stratford-on-Jhelum look. Timbered balconies seem like architectural postscripts.

The city has run down at the heels since the British left. The polo fields and tennis court are deep in weeds. The billiard table in my hotel was ripped. Toilets had ceased to flush. Electric lights were feeble. The flower-decked six-room houseboats where the British lived are weather-beaten hulks. The faded "Chatham Walk," "Queen Mary," "Piccadilly" are memories of better days. My visit to the famous Shalimar Gardens was a great disappointment. Its canals had dried up, its flower beds were overgrown and untrimmed. Egg shells and cigarette butts littered the walks. Starving dogs assaulted my picnic lunch. Beggars refused to leave until I paid them.

The only well-fed Asiatics I saw in Kashmir were the wide, red-faced Kazaks. The burly Communist fighters, in their long fur garments, felt boots and skull caps, were arriving by plane-loads. They looked like people out of *Lost Horizon*. They gaped in awe at the wretched town which, to them, was a great metropolis.

Kashmir was a Paradise in full decay. I was tantalized during my whole stay by the beauty of its mountains which I could never enjoy simply because some desperate merchant's face was always poked into mine.

Kashmir's people lean toward their Mohammedan brethren in Pakistan. But the country is ruled by Sheik Abdullah, supported by Indian bayonets. This political schizophrenia is dangerous. The *Pale Hands Behind The Shalimar* well may trigger a machine gun that could start a war between its rival political suitors.

Pakistan

Peshawar's bazaars topped any I had seen thus far in the East. Swaggerers in rags who lived out of bundles sought the frontiers of Paradise in the Street of the Maidens. The fingers and toes of the veiled girls were hennaed. Tall Afridi and Swati carried rifles with ivory inlaid stocks. The Street of the Story Tellers was heavy with traffic of green-turbaned Mullahs, iron-brown Wazaris and fierce Pathans accompanied by little boys in velvet dress.

Old men sat on balconies sucking water pipes. The heavy smell of camel dung floated in the air. Dancing boys, with roses behind their ears and their eyes painted with collyrium, flirted with hawk-nosed tribesmen. One tossed me a rose. Turbaned men with the red beards that pronounced their having made the pilgrimage to Mecca bought gold-thread slippers and bargained with the coppersmiths.

Dogs snarled and fought in narrow alleys. Donkeys and camels were tethered in streets and courtyards of this Central Asia caravansary. There were hopping beggars, their arms and faces eaten away by leprosy.

I drank whiskey with the American consul in the Peshawar Club, in the paneled bar hung with pictures of British army hunt masters. The stacks of *Punch* and *Sketch* in the library dated up

to 1947. A list of British captains and majors, whose names had been posted for nonpayment of 1947 club dues, still hung on the wall of the entrance hall.

The consul told me that Pakistan was the most hopeful of the countries of southern Asia.

"It is the country most worth cultivating in this part of the world," he said. "Despite the fact it got off to a late start, it is the most modern country here. The Mohammedans have a northern vigor in contrast to the sun-enervated Hindus. Religion does not get in the way of progress here as it does in India."

The other Americans I met in Pakistan and other parts of the East were to concur with this opinion. They shared the consul's admiration of Pakistan's progressive character.

The main feature of my visit to Pakistan was the trip I made through the Khyber Pass on my way to Afghanistan. It was the realization of a dream I had held since boyhood. It was one of the great romantic places in the world to me, the synonym for military adventure.

We entered the military highway to the Khyber Pass at dawn. Our crossing of the Peshawar Plain was swift. Within a few minutes, we were over the Indus River. Our papers were triple-checked at Fort Jamrud even though we were riding in the embassy station wagon, and we mounted the winding roads of the Pass. The Northwest Frontier is still a no-man's land but the road is neutral territory, patrolled through its length by Pakistan soldiers.

Below the auto road wound the road reserved for donkey and camel traffic. We passed caravans of hairy plodding Bactrian camels, piled with carpet-wrapped swaying bundles. Flat-faced Uzbegs returning from their pilgrimages to Mecca rode shaggy ponies. There were Tartars and Turkomans on their way to the fleshpots of Peshawar. I saw blind people being led by ropes.

One camel bore a Wazari's harem on a platform. Women carrying jars and bundles of faggots on their heads drew black cloaks over their eyes as we passed small fortified villages. They wore baggy pantaloons. Though men off the road are fair game, the tribesmen consider it a disgrace to shoot a woman—hence the red pants which serve as deer-hunters' red jackets do in American forests.

We stopped at a village of mud- and stone-constructed huts for tea. To get to our host's house, we had to dive through a series of trenches. If we had been above ground off the road, we might have been shot by a rifle from one of the opposite village's sniping towers. These villages participate in father-to-son blood feuds like those of Kentuckians.

The domestic fortress houses are built on several levels, Casbah fashion. In the courtyard I saw goats being decapitated. On another level, women cooked. On the roof (which I visited cautiously), brown-turbaned men and boys poked rifles into slits, watching neighboring houses. The untamed highlanders were friendly. They seemed to lead a warrior existence without benefit of schools, taxes or law courts. They were proud of their rifles. They showed me Lee Enfields and Martinis and long-barreled muskets with hand-whittled stocks. A basket held homemade hand grenades. The only factory in the Pass is, appropriately enough, a rifle factory.

Their violence extends to the settling of domestic problems within the home. The nose of one of the women who was cooking seemed singularly wrong for her face. It was fleshier than their normal aquiline-shaped noses are, and the texture seemed strange. My interpreter told me that tribesmen punish straying wives by cutting their noses off. Back in the British days, an enterprising merchant imported artificial noses from England to sell to wayward tribeswomen who wished to hide their disgrace. He had obviously had great difficulty, however, in matching size and color.

As we drove higher in the Pass, we left the villages behind us. On a peak above we had a glimpse of Fort Maude, looking like a medieval stronghold. British regimental crests on cliff faces were memorials, reminding us that every mile of the Pass we traveled on had been paid for in British blood. Their dates ran from the middle of the 19th century to 1947. I recognized the crests of the Argyle and Southern Highlanders, units of whom I had met in Korea. I also recognized the Essex and Cheshires.

Jagged red rocks reached over the Ali Masjid Gorge, narrowest part of the Pass. As we flashed through it, I could visualize a column of white-helmeted, red-jacketed Tommy Atkinses ambushed by battle-loving Sons of the Prophet.

The skirling of pipes was drowned by bounding boulders and volleys of bullets. At the last fort, we left the green and white crescent flag of Pakistan behind us.

Afghanistan

Afghanistan was a brutal, forbidding land. The Khyber Pass opened onto a desert rimmed with gray mountains. Overhead a copper-colored sky flamed. The road bed was barely distinguishable from the plain. Only higher piles of razor-sharp rocks and marker slabs distinguished it. Most of

our navigation was, of necessity, in low gear. Tires perished with sick hisses and wheel hubs, catching in sand, necessitated getting out and shoveling.

A sudden dust storm brought the caravans to a halt. The camels knelt and their drivers sheltered behind them. Beyond the city of Jellahabad, we met masses of nomads on their annual migration to India from the Oxus.

Dirty, evil-looking men in sheepskin coats and turbans led contemptuous, rubber-necking camels, carrying bales of tents and rugs and pots, pans and glowing copper samovars as well as chickens and baby lambs. At water holes, swarthy challenging-eyed women with leather-dry skins and talon-like fingers pulled at my clothes and beard, taking cigarettes, candy, money, hard-boiled eggs, anything. The babies that were tied to donkeys were covered with sores which were in turn covered with flies. Their red eyes were filled with pus. Some were blind from trachoma.

Two hundred thousand Kuchis make the long trip from Siberia over mountain passes and deserts to India each fall. They need the grass for their flocks and earn money by digging wells and begging along the Grand Trunk Road. In the spring, India's consuming sun burns the grass and they drive north over the route by which they came to green pasture lands on foot and on camel. They float across the rivers on inflated goatskins.

Night swallowed the plain soon after we met the Kuchis. We passed them all through the night where they had pitched their black goatskin-hair tents and built large bonfires, against the scarlet light of which the humped shapes of camels were silhouetted. The harsh defiles of the mountain spur we had to cross before we reached Kabul was filled with the nomads. Droves of goats butted at the station wagon while we waited for them to pass.

Kabul itself was black. There was no one abroad other than the Gestapo-like uniformed police the headlights picked up at corners. The station wagon dropped me at the Hotel Kabul. I spent the night alone except for lizards snapping at flies and making love on the walls in a room bare except for a bedstead.

By day, Kabul was anything but prepossessing. Its white buildings were one or two stories high with flat roofs and no windows. Lines of ragged peasant recruits wearing blanket rolls marched gapingly through the center of town on their way to the barracks. Khaki-clad cavalry men posted with jingles through the mud.

All of the women were in purdah—purple, blue, pink and white pleated ground-scraping shrouds that hid their feminine charms. I did not see one woman's face during my stay in Kabul.

Kabul's bazaars were even more exotic than those of Peshawar. My senses reacted violently to the deafening, sprawling scene; to the stench of sweating men and animals, of baking and cooking, of donkey and camel dung. There was a motley, brawling crowd of Hazars, Tajiks, Swatis and Afridis, Turkomans from Bokhara and Samarkand. They went about barefoot or in leather sandals with upturned toes, carrying rifles, sometimes with their sashes filled with daggers and pistols. White camel caravans from Kandahar and Herat towered over the crowd.

I was startled by a certain incongruity of costume. At least one out of every four of the Central Asiatic tribesmen wore an American army officer's blouse complete with eagle buttons, insignia, divisional patches and lieutenant and captain's bars. This along with turbans, baggy pants and turned-up-toe sandals. The blouses, which were on sale in all the shops of the clothing bazaar, had found their way overland from Persia after World War II. It's what the well-dressed tribesman is wearing in Afghanistan today!

I drank tea with a fat Bokhara rug vendor. We squatted on the open platform of his shop with a curious crowd watching. They laughed loudly when I declined a suck at the vendor's hubble-bubble pipe.

I was invited by a friendly Afridi to eat pink sherbet on green leaves of rice and mutton mixture. I accepted the sherbet and skipped the rice and mutton, as well as thumb-sized grapes

and figs which were festooned with clouds of black flies. The bazaar was noisy, almost as though a half dozen modern symphonies were being played simultaneously. Sheep were being slaughtered by the hundred in the Street of the Butchers. They contributed a piteous bleating chorus. Donkey drivers cursed. The tin- and blacksmiths hammered at forges and the silversmiths tapped at necklaces and fake ancient Greek coins. Blind minstrels wailed. Flutes piped from the roofs. As if there were not color enough in the bazaar, men from the Street of the Dyers, their arms and legs dyed from their work, provided stabs of brilliant green and red.

My sketchbooks were jammed with drawings.

I spent the last of the country's currency that I carried on Lucky Strikes in green packages. They had evidently been on the shelves before "Lucky Strike went to war." I tried them but soon gave up. I used them as parting presents to Afghanis. They conspicuously did not thank me.

Afghanistan is a buffer state between Soviet Russia and the countries of South Asia. However, after seeing the pathetically ill-equipped soldiers (flyers without planes, infantrymen without artillery), I was convinced that the country would be a push-over in case of a Russian invasion. Brave hearts and rifles are hardly stoppers for tanks and jets.

Turkey

The appearance of a Shriner from Des Moines, Iowa, would probably start a riot in the streets of Istanbul. Modern Turkey has abandoned the fez and the veil, along with outmoded feudal patterns of life.

The Turks are devoted to the ideal of freedom. The rugged soldiers of the country are ready to die in its defense. Every man in Turkey serves a period in the army. It's a nation of trained soldiers: no one is exempted from military service. There is no such thing as a 4-F classification. Even midgets are conscripted. I saw a platoon of them drilling. I also saw one-eyed and one-armed Turkish GI's.

America is pouring in money and weapons to streamline the Turkish army. Every nickel of the taxpayer's money is well spent here.

Major General Arnold, head of the U. S. Military Mission in Turkey, was enthusiastic about the Turkish soldiers.

"There are none better than the tough Turks," he told me. "They've been fighting the Russians for 800 years and have never been conquered by them. They are used to the rigors of a hard existence. As children, they run barefoot in the snow. They acclimate themselves immediately to the worst conditions—they can take anything. They are the most rugged men in the world. If the Russians ever try to invade Turkey, you can be sure there will be a million bloody Turkish bayonets."

I felt Turkey was the most enheartening country I had seen in Asia. I was glad that her million bayonets were definitely on our side.

Asia was over for me. I stopped at Rome to worship Michelangelo's ceiling in the Sistine Chapel and at Paris to look into the enigmatic eyes of the *Mona Lisa* once again. A few days later, I limped gratefully into my New York studio.

Mayr Donald Strand   Col James M Brown

Hot Jazz in the Indian Barracks

Gen MacArthur